Empowering Your Life
with
ANGELS

Empowering Your Life with ANGELS

Rita S. Berkowitz

with

Deborah S. Romaine

ALPHA

A member of Penguin Group (USA) Inc.

Publisher: Marie Butler-Knight
Product Manager: Phil Kitchel
Senior Managing Editor: Jennifer Chisholm
Senior Acquisitions Editor: Randy Ladenheim-Gil
Book Producer: Lee Ann Chearney/Amaranth Illuminare
Development Editor: Christy Wagner
Production Editor: Janette Lynn
Copy Editor: Nancy Wagner
Cover Designer: Bill Thomas
Book Designer: Trina Wurst
Creative Director: Robin Lasek
Indexer: Angie Bess
Proofreader: Angela Calvert, Mary Hunt

To our readers: As you breathe deeply in and out, may you feel the brush of angel wings beating from your heart.

Contents

Introduction

The Kabbalah tells us "over every blade of grass an angel floats, whispering, 'Grow!'" Grow! This is the same message your angels and guides have for you as they soar around you and surround you in Divine energy, light, and love. Grow in enlightenment, comfort, and joy. Grow in wisdom and compassion. *Grow.* This is what your angels and guides want for *you* as a spiritual being that is as much of the Divine as are they. After all, we each belong to the whole of the Universe and all its energy. We—you—are of the Divine just as the Divine is of us.

As an ordained minister and certified medium in the Spiritualist Church who was raised in the Jewish faith, I have what people have told me is a rather unique perspective on the Divine and its many emissaries that take the forms of angels, spirit guides, and people living here on the earth plane. When you believe we are all one and that we are all one with the Divine, as I do, *anything* becomes possible. You must do your part to manifest your dreams and hopes, of course. There's a bit of work involved, and it is up to you to do your work. But your angels and your guides are here to help you learn the lessons your soul has entered this life to learn … and to experience joy, love, and contentment along the way.

In my work as a spirit artist, I draw the visual images that present themselves to me when I connect with Spirit. Often these are images of loved ones who have passed to the higher side, and when they appear in such recognizable form, they often bring unspeakable joy and comfort to their loved ones who remain here on the earth plane. Other times the images are of angelic beings and beings of spirit who are here to guide and nurture us. We all need reassurance, at times, that there is a bigger whole … and that we are part of it. One of my great joys in my work is being able to help connect people with this wholeness in ways that are personally and uniquely meaningful to them. You'll see some of my spirit drawings and other artwork in the illustrations that appear throughout this book.

In my work as a medium, I have had the privilege to experience Spirit as pure light and energy, an experience that is different each time and one that defies description. There are no words. This is an odd statement to make in a book, I know. I can say only that it is truly an amazing, uplifting, and awesome experience. You, too, can touch the angels and experience Spirit and the Divine. *We all can.* I'll show you how through the many interactive exercises in each chapter, and you'll see how an experience can be worth a thousand words!

And I have known many, many "earth angels" in my life, people who come into the picture at just the right time with just the right "stuff" to allow my path to unfold and my dreams to manifest. You'll meet some of these wonderful individuals as you read this book. Also in this book you'll meet angels ancient and contemporary, mythical and ordinary, religious and secular, ethereal and earthly. Interactive exercises will show you how to connect with angels who might already be familiar to you as well as angels who are simply there to help you when you call upon them. This help is endless, abundant, and generous; all you have to do is ask.

Learning and exploring should be fun, right? Of course! So to help this book be fun for you as you're learning about angels and guides and exploring your unique connections with the Divine, you're going to make a set of angel meditation cards. Each chapter has an exercise to make a unique card, and I draw from my experience as an artist to give you guidance and suggestions for creating cards that express meanings personal for you. In the final chapter, Chapter 12, you'll bring your set of cards together in a culminating exercise that will reveal the most amazing angel of all—*the angel within you.*

Whether your orientation to angels and guides comes from your faith and beliefs, your curiosity, your hope, or your quest for knowledge and understanding, *Empowering Your Life with Angels* will show you how you can draw guidance, support, and encouragement from the Divine energy that is here for each of us.

In light and love,
Rita Berkowitz

Part 1

Angels All Around You: What Is True

In the 1988 movie *Wings of Desire* and its 1998 remake *City of Angels,* angels are everywhere. We, the audience, see them hovering above buildings and sitting on the shoulders of statues in the parks. The characters in these movies don't see or notice the angels all around them although they do often experience their subtle interventions. Emissaries of the Divine, the movie angels watch and witness, take notes, and walk among those on the earth plane to offer comfort, solace, and suggestion. It doesn't matter to these angels whether the people they help believe in them; they help anyway. This is why angels are here.

Angels are all around us in real life. They walk with us and are ready to respond when we ask (consciously or through our higher selves) for their help and guidance. The angels in real life take many forms, both ethereal and physical. Your angels might be the spirits of loved ones on the higher side, strangers you encounter at opportune moments, or friends who are with you in difficult times. Seen and unseen, there are angels watching over you right now, and they want to help you. All you have to do is ask. It's easier than you might think!

Some things are true whether you believe in them or not.
—Angel Seth (played by Nicolas Cage) in *City of Angels* (1998)

Chapter 1

Why We Believe in Angels and They Believe in Us

How many angels touched your life today? Angels take many shapes and forms—some familiar, some otherworldly, and some we don't even recognize as angels. The angels in our lives may be corporeal—having tangible bodies, living among us as people we know or strangers we encounter. Or they may be ethereal—splashes of light, shapes of shadow, perhaps even beatific beings complete with halos and gossamer wings.

There are countless concepts of what—or who—angels are. Some people believe angels are beings so pure that they have no reason to incarnate, but remain as energy forms that appear as brilliant light. Other people believe angels are entities from other universes that populated our Earth and now look over us. And still others believe angels are loved ones who have passed and remain present as personal angels who safeguard them. From mythology's winged messengers of the gods, to the Kabbalah's viewpoint that every idea is an angel, to the Bible's hierarchy of angels, to ordinary people who appear at just the right time to perform extraordinary actions, angels populate every culture and every belief system throughout the history of humankind.

No matter what or how we perceive angels to be, we experience them all around us, every day. Angels bring us guidance, assistance, comfort, peace, light, faith, and hope. They remind us that there is a divine order to the Universe that supports our existence and our lifepaths. Perhaps your awareness of angels is strongest when you are troubled, sad, in danger, or facing major life decisions or challenges. Maybe you sense angelic energy surround you when you get in your car or board an airplane. Or maybe you know angels are always there, just like the air you breathe.

Every one of us is part of the higher realm, the realm of spirits and angels and the Divine. We are not just connected to this realm individually by some sort of a cosmic string or a thought.

We are connected to *a whole*. When we look at the beautiful Spirit of this, when we look at each and every one of the beautiful souls—and of how we are one in truth—then we understand that we are *all* part of the whole. The angels are not separate from us nor we from them. All exist together as one, on the earth plane and in the higher realm. Angels are those who touch our lives in ways that we may or may not recognize, whether we ask them to do so or whether we avoid their gaze.

If the doors of perception were cleansed, everything would appear to man as it is, infinite.

—William Blake (1757–1827), English poet and artist

I want to open you to the abilities you have within you to experience the presence of angels in your life—and to the possibilities this experience opens to you. My angels have changed my life, and I know your angels, whether or not you recognize them, have changed yours. This is, after all, why angels come to us.

In this book, I share with you my experiences as well as the experiences of others that affirm and demonstrate the presence and actions of angels. I do this from within the framework of my lifework as a healer, psychic medium, counselor, and artist with utmost respect for, though without bias toward, specific religious teachings and belief systems. I encourage you, as you read this book, to interpret and apply information within the framework of *your* lifework and beliefs. If something I say doesn't quite fit your perceptions, take a few minutes to think it through. What doesn't fit and why? Take the information as you might a lump of clay, and shape it into forms that make sense to you. Use the message of this book in the way that works for you—empowerment comes when you make it your own.

Each chapter contains exercises and activities to introduce you to the angels in your life and to show you how to communicate with them to encourage and support your *highest and best*. This term, *highest and best*, is one you'll hear me use often; it refers to what is right for you as you travel the path of your destiny in this life. (It also identifies extended exercises and activities throughout this book.) Angels are not here to give you what you ask for—they're not genies granting you wishes! Rather, angels are here to provide guidance, direction, assistance, assurance, comfort, and protection in ways that help you grow and evolve spiritually. Sometimes what we want right now is not what is right for our paths, even when it seems so to us. Angels help us manifest what is right for our lives. This is part of the great joy of awareness, of *knowing* the presence of angels. This is how we experience the Divine in our lives.

Light Works: Create a Sacred Space

Some people like to create a sacred space for meditation, prayer, or however they choose to communicate with the Divine, to keep the energy pure for connecting with their angels and spirit guides in the higher realm. If you're so inclined, create such a space in your home that you use for nothing else but your meditations. It needn't be a large or elaborate space, just a space in which you feel comfortable and can be undisturbed. Some people choose to put imagery of spiritual significance in this space; some people choose to place crystals and fragrances; some people choose to keep the space absolutely clear. Do whatever feels right to you.

And of course, you can create a sacred space wherever you happen to be simply by forming the intent to communicate with your angels. You can be lying on the couch, sitting in your garden, even driving in your car. You don't have to be in your sacred space to contact your angels; your sacred space simply gives you a special place of retreat and sanctity.

In the Presence of Angels

I've always known someone was watching over me, even when I was a young child and a teen. I escaped a lot of the things that happened to my friends because I was always pushed to where I was supposed to be. Now, as a medium and spirit artist, I am blessed to be aware of the presence of angels perhaps more than the average person is. What

I connect to as the angelic form is the pure energy of who and what we are. There are times when angels appear to me as absolutely beautiful images; other times as light; and still other times as Italian grandmothers, Hassidic rabbis (as one of my own angels appears), Native American dancers, and Asian herbalists.

An angel has a purpose, a reason for bringing help. It's not just that angels are here. Whether it comes as a winged being as the Renaissance paintings portray, a loved one passed to spirit, or someone who walks into our lives, the angelic form brings us energy when we have the need. We might not be aware we need help or we're asking for help, but our higher selves know and they ask on our behalf.

In the Light: Why Do *You* Believe in Angels?

Each of us has our own personal and spiritual foundations for believing in angels. For the most part, however, we believe in angels because we feel their presence and influences in our lives. Angels help us, guide us, and comfort us. Why do *you* believe in angels? Take a few minutes to think about it, if you need to, then write down some of your reasons:

I believe in angels because:

_____

_____

_____

The first time I became aware of an angelic presence in my life was:

_____

_____

_____

The most recent or most memorable experience I had involving an angel was:

_____

_____

_____

Read your responses out loud. What images and feelings come to you when you hear your beliefs and experiences expressed through your own words?

Angels in Spirit

People come to me to connect with loved ones who have passed to the higher side. Their reasons for doing so are as varied as the people themselves. For some of them, I draw the loved one who appears; for others, I convey messages of comfort and love. For some people, this process provides closure; for others, it is an awakening of sorts, an affirmation that there is "more" beyond physical existence. It is amazing work, and it brings me great joy.

When a spirit comes from the higher side with a message, it's always special for the loved one receiving it, although it's not necessarily angelic. But when there's a purpose to the message, a reason to help, that spirit is serving in the role of an angel.

Gail, a woman in her mid-40s, had a close relationship with her father, and after he passed to the higher side, Gail often felt his presence around her. She lived alone, and one day, as she was doing some cleaning, she heard her father's voice. His words were clear and distinct: "Lock the doors! Call the police!"

Alarmed, Gail stopped what she was doing and walked through the rooms of her house. When she looked out the kitchen window, she noticed a man, someone she did not know, approaching the barn about a hundred yards from her house. She ran into the dining room and looked out another window. She did not see the man, but the barn door was open. Gail heard her father's voice again, saying with great urgency, "Call the police!"

Gail could feel her father's presence very strongly and knew she was in danger. She locked her front and back doors, closed the window blinds, and telephoned the police. As happens in small towns such as the one in which Gail lived, the police came immediately. As they arrived, they encountered the man walking from the barn toward the house, a piece of metal pipe in his hands. As the police arrested him, Gail realized her father's message from the higher side probably saved her life. Gail's father became an angel in her life.

Earth Angels

Angels often take the form of people in our everyday lives, too. They might appear as individuals we know or strangers we encounter who bring us just the kind of help we need just when we need it ... and often when we least expect it. I believe Spirit guides these Earth angels to us just when we need them.

One such angel who touched my life at just the right time and changed its course was Mrs. Brown, my ninth-grade art teacher at W. Arthur Cunningham Junior High School in Brooklyn, New York. Mrs. Brown saw that I had somewhat of a gift in art, and one day before lunch, she approached me and said, "Rita, I want you to develop this gift," and she gave me an application form for the High School of Art and Design in Manhattan. The only catch was that the form had to be completed, signed by a parent, and brought back that same day.

So I had to take it home right then, during my lunchtime. My dad was not home, of course, as it was the middle of the day, so my mom filled out the form. She was not as difficult to convince as my dad would have been that this was the right thing for me to do. It meant going to high school away from my neighborhood, and it was a major letting-go for my parents to allow me to do this.

Mrs. Brown was the angel who came forward to say, "Do it, do it now!" I was able to run home, fill out the form with my mother, and get it back to the school. I went to the High School of Art and Design and then on to the Pratt Institute, which helped direct me in my art career.

The Kabbalah, ancient Jewish mysticism, says that every idea forms a ball of energy and that ball of energy becomes an angel. One such ball of energy that entered my life was Eva, who became a dear friend. Eva moved into a studio a few doors down from mine—and into my life— in 1980. One day she walked down the hallway, stuck her head in my doorway with a beautiful smile on her face, and said, "Hey, want to start a gallery?" Then she stepped back.

I did want to start a gallery. Eva's gentle prodding was what I needed to get going, and together we started The Loading Dock Gallery. It was the first of many times in my life that Eva would plant the seeds of change and then step back to let them grow. Later, we laughingly joked that Eva came up with the ideas and allowed the rest of us to do all the work. But Eva was the thought that became an angel. She was that angel who came in and touched lives, then stepped back. She didn't try to control events; she just let them happen.

On May 29, 2003, Eva passed to the higher side. She had been ill for some time and knew the time of her passing was near. She had told her best friend that she wanted me to do her memorial service. Her friend, knowing how busy my schedule is, asked Eva, "Have you talked to Rita about this?" Eva just smiled and said, "Don't worry about it."

On the morning of May 29, I was at the gym, as is my Thursday schedule. There was someone new on the exercise cycle across from me, wearing sunglasses while working out—if that's what you could call her leisurely pace. I laughed to myself because the woman looked just like Eva, and "just like Eva" did not appear fond of physical exertion. The woman looked at me and smiled—unusual behavior in a gym where interchanges between people typically consist of polite greetings but no real interaction. Each time during the hour or so I was there, whenever I looked over at this woman who was exercising in half-time, she smiled at me. *I have to tell Eva her father must've had another child, because this woman looks and acts so much like her she could be her sister,* I thought to myself.

When I left the gym, I immediately called Eva from my cell phone before heading to my office. I knew once my day got underway I would not have time to call, and I was excited to tell Eva about the woman in the gym. "Eva?" I said when a woman answered the phone. "No, this is Wendy," was the reply. Wendy, Eva's best friend, told me Eva had passed to the higher side about an hour earlier. She then asked me if I would do the service as Eva had wanted.

I was stunned; had I not seen the woman in the gym, I would have gone straight to my office and then to the evening class I was teaching. I would have not learned of Eva's passing until late at night, by which time it would have become a scramble to accommodate the service.

I was able to do the service, and it was beautiful—just what Eva had wanted. We all could feel that she was pleased. But Eva had one more angelic mission. Eva had left her house and her possessions to Wendy, who had cared for Eva during her extended illness. Among those possessions was Eva's mother's engagement ring, which Eva's family wanted back. Wendy was more than willing to return the ring, but she couldn't find it. After searching the house for several hours, Wendy threw her hands to the heavens. "Eva, where is the ring?" she implored. "Your family really wants it, and I have no idea where to look."

Clearly and distinctly, Wendy heard a voice—although she couldn't say it was Eva's—tell her, "Go out on the back porch. There is a small cardboard box. The ring is there." Wendy did as the voice directed. Sure enough, there on the back porch was a small box ... and in the box was the ring. Wendy was pleased and relieved to give the ring to Eva's family.

In the Light: Thank Your Angels!

This is a good time to take a moment to offer a quick "thanks" to the angels in your life. And it's a good idea to set aside a brief time each day to thank the angels who make your life, and your lifepath, a little bit easier. Give tangible thanks, now and again, to your tangible angels—send a card, give a flower, or leave a note. They won't be expecting it, which makes it all the more meaningful! And send a prayer or meditation of gratitude to your spirit angels just to let them know you feel and appreciate their presence and assistance. Gratitude is sending love back to the angels.

Angels of Passage

Angels frequently appear to people as they approach the time of passage to the higher side—their moment of physical death. As a minister and a healer, I am often with people as they approach the time of their passing, and often when I am with them at this time, I see angels. One such experience that was at once moving and comforting was when I was with my very dear friend Eric, who had been ill for quite a few years. Eric was in hospice, and I was giving him healing in the form of a foot massage.

As I touched Eric's feet, I closed my eyes. Much to my surprise, from behind the head of the bed I saw the most glorious angel. She was wearing red tapestry and looked as though she had just stepped from a medieval painting. I recognized that this was coming from a different religious background than mine, and I knew she was there just for Eric. The angel spread her wings around the bed until she totally surrounded the bed and the tip of her wings touched at the foot of the bed where I was sitting. At that moment, I became fully aware that my friend was about to be taken to the higher side. I knew Eric was protected, that this wondrous angel was taking care of him, that she watched over him. And I knew Eric was aware of the angel's presence and it gave him comfort and peace.

When I completed the healing, I stepped away from the bed. I'd been with Eric for several hours and I felt tired; I left the room to go out for a cup of tea. When I returned to the room, Eric had slipped into a coma. He passed two days later.

This might sound like a sad story, a story of loss, but it really is a story of joy. I felt the angel protecting my friend, and I knew he would be safe, and feel safe, on his passage to the higher side. To know his safety is a blessing of comfort I will never forget.

Words were originally magic, and to this day, words have retained much of their ancient magical power.
—Sigmund Freud (1856–1939), psychoanalyst

Light Works: Make Your Own Angel Cards

You've probably seen angel cards in stores that sell metaphysical and inspirational items. These cards come in various sizes and styles, and most feature a word and an accompanying illustration. You can use angel cards for inspiration and guidance in your meditations. Some people choose a new card each morning and focus intently throughout the day to put the word's concept into practice. Some people select cards during times of stress to provide comfort or encouragement. And some people pick cards for affirmations. There are many ways to use angel cards.

As part of learning to empower your life with angels, you're going to make your own angel cards. In each chapter, I'll give you a word for the angel card and some comments about it, presented in a shaded box (the first of which follows this section). Write the word on material of your choosing, then illustrate the word in some way. You may draw or cut out pictures or symbols, add items, or simply color the letters of the word. You don't have to be an artist—just create images that have meaning for you. Give this some thought before you start. Materials you might consider using include the following:

- Colored inks or markers
- Colored paper or cardboard
- Feathers
- Found images (photos, magazine pictures)
- Paints
- Pieces of fabric or leather
- Slats of wood
- Small beads
- Small tiles
- Stones large enough to contain a word

Be creative! Choose materials that have meaning for you in the context of angel communication, your personal spirit connections, and your beliefs.

Before you make the angel card for each chapter, explore the word with all your senses—how does it look, sound, feel, smell, and even taste? As you write the word, let your whole self—body, mind, and spirit—experience the letters as you form them. Then create an image that represents what the word means to you. When you finish the card, hold it in your hands.

Create a container for your angel cards, too, something to hold and protect them when you are not using them. This might be a box you construct or decorate, a fabric bag you make, a piece of pottery, etc. At the end of the book, you'll have 12 angel cards. In each chapter, I'll provide a suggested meditation or other use for the chapter's card. The final exercise in Chapter 12 will pull your angel cards together in a conclusion.

Light Works: Chapter 1 Angel Card

This chapter's angel card word is *Oneness*. It is common when first beginning to work with angels to think of them as entities separate from us humans. Yet they are of us, and we are of them. We might think of ourselves as separate from the Divine, from the angelic, from Spirit. But we are not. We are all one through energy, as we are one energy.

Using the materials you've selected, write this word—*Oneness*—and illustrate it to create your first angel card.

Why Angels Come to Help You

None of us here on the earth plane has the inside scoop on the master plan, the grand design, of existence. However, each of us negotiated our roles in the unfoldment of that plan before entering the earth plane. The result is your destiny, the opportunities you have chosen to learn the lessons your soul needs to complete—your lifepath. Once here, you choose how to follow your lifepath. I and only I am accountable for my lifepath; you and only you are accountable for yours—although we are not alone in making our choices and decisions. Available to each of us, like an endless sea of resources, is the infinite and divine wisdom of the Universe. All we need to do is ask, and what we need (although, again, not necessarily what we *want*) is ours. Angels are the messengers that bring to us, and connect us to, the Divine.

An angel who connects me to the Divine is Issaiah, a rabbi who lived in biblical times. I became aware that he walked with me when I was just eight or nine years old, although I didn't know who he was until years later. Now, looking back on my childhood, I recognize that Issaiah drew me to religious philosophy. As a child, I would walk to the Orthodox synagogue and sit in the women's section to listen to the men pray—not such a common thing for a young girl to do. I was drawn not because of Judaism, but because of the intense spiritual energy I felt when I was sitting there.

Many years later, I recognized that this presence I felt was an angel sent to guide me, and as is usual for me, I had to put my recognition into a visual form. I painted the image of this rabbi spirit guide, similar to the black-and-white drawing that appears here. He had wonderful features and a warm, compassionate face, and I was pleased to see him on canvas. About six months after I did the painting, I was sitting in circle (a gathering in which a medium does readings) and the medium came over to me. "Issaiah is with you," she said and described my rabbi. It was the first time I'd heard his name from another medium. What a marvelous validation that was!

Issaiah, Rita's spirit rabbi.

13

Today, when I function in spiritual contexts such as in church or when I am teaching mediumship classes, I open my mouth to speak and I feel an energy shift happen. I feel my throat open and the words come out. I speak without preparation, and what I say turns out to be what people need to hear. I trust in it, in Issaiah's guidance, and it always works.

Life Lessons

Following your path in life is a bit like playing the piano. When you're doing it right, it feels right. When you're not, it's like hitting the wrong notes. They might be jarringly dissonant or gently off-key, but you know they're the wrong notes. Each of us agrees to this path before we come here. It's decided *with* us, not *for* us. But when we get here, we need the angels in our lives to remind us that we're doing what we're supposed to be doing. Sometimes what feels like the wrong path is simply paving the way for another. Angels help us stay on our paths. They encourage us when we're doing what we're supposed to be doing and gently (and sometimes not so gently!) nudge us back on track when we stray.

Remember I said earlier in this chapter that angels sometimes appear to me as Italian grandmothers? One who did so was Vennera, great-grandmother of our book producer Lee Ann. I was doing a reading for Lee Ann, and quite a number of spirits came to make contact. When Lee Ann asked me to draw one of them, they all became very still and it felt like they stepped aside for a woman to come through. It was clear I was to draw this woman. She presented in her later years, a strong woman with a gentle, loving face. As I often do, I was talking to Lee Ann while I drew, sharing with her the guidance and direction this spirit was giving me. I was working in color, and the woman instructed me to color the sky a beautiful blue with hints of orange. This, she said, was to help Lee Ann recognize this time as a new dawn in her life, a dawn of happiness, of hope and encouragement.

Lee Ann suspected the woman in the drawing was her maternal great-grandmother Vennera, but there were no pictures of Vennera to confirm her belief. At this time in her life, Lee Ann was the primary caregiver for her 94-year-old grandmother, Jessie, Vennera's daughter. Lee Ann took the drawing to Jessie and asked her if she knew who it was. Jessie studied the drawing for a few minutes, then playfully touched the nose of the drawing. "Jessie!" she said, her own name, and she laughed.

Lee Ann's great-grandmother Vennera.

Lee Ann last saw her grandmother a year later, just before Jessie passed to the higher side. As Lee Ann bent down to give her beloved grandmother a kiss, Jessie reached up with a shaky finger and touched Lee Ann's face. "Jessie," she said. Now Lee Ann often senses the presence of these two strong and loving Sicilian women, one she never met and one she knew quite well, guiding and informing her life.

Soul Lessons

We, of course, benefit from the intervention and guidance of angels. But why do angels choose to interact with us? How do angels benefit from how they help us? The assistance given to us by those on the higher side—spirit guides and loved ones who have passed—helps them in their own evolution. The lessons our souls are learning continue without boundaries, whether on the earth plane or the higher side. For spirit guides, intervention helps them maintain their knowledge and skills they acquired while on the earth plane.

As much as any other reason, it seems that angels want to help us just for the pure and simple joy of it. Think of this generosity in terms of your own experiences: You've no doubt given a gift to someone—friend, child, sibling, partner—that was totally unexpected and that you knew was exactly what the person wanted. Even now you probably can picture the expression of delight and surprise that lit up the person's face as the wrapping paper fell away. Sometimes we all like to do things for others for the sheer and sole pleasure of giving, and this appears to be the case with angels, as well.

That best portion of a good man's life, his little, nameless, unremembered acts of kindness and of love.
—William Wordsworth (1770–1850), English poet

Highest and Best: Reaching Out to Your Angels

Your angels are available to help you when you need them, and you don't have to wait for them to offer their assistance. You can—and should—go to them for guidance. This meditation exercise can help you connect with your angels. This is a lengthy exercise, so I suggest you read it all the way through first. Consider reading it aloud (or having someone whose voice you enjoy hearing read it aloud to you) and tape-recording it, then playing the tape to follow as a guided meditation.

1. Go to your sacred space or a place in the house where you will not be disturbed. Make yourself comfortable. Light scented candles or incense if you like.

2. Start out by taking three slow, deep breaths, in through your nose and out through your mouth. Allow your first breath to clear your body. With your second breath, open your mind. With your third breath, free your spirit.

3. Remind yourself that this is your time to connect with the god of your beliefs. You are god's perfect child (the god of your understanding), and this is an opportunity for you to grow to reach your full potential.

4. Visualize yourself as a flower just breaking through the earth on a beautiful spring day. The cold of winter has gone away, the earth is just beginning to get soft, and a young tulip is breaking through. Feel that energy of the push to break the surface. Feel the energy of reaching for the warmth of the light. Feel yourself open to grow.

5. As you reach higher, visualize yourself as a beautiful lavender tulip opening. As you visualize that flower, opening slowly petal by petal, visualize that you can connect to all that is. Feel the energy from the open flower connecting with the light, and on that beam of light, let yourself rise to the higher realm with the intent that you are going to those who watch over you.

6. As you go past the trees, past the clouds, and out into the stars, ask that your most high guides, your most beautiful angels, come to you. Allow them to see you. Allow them to touch your life. Even more, allow yourself to be touched.

7. Ask them any question you have, and trust in the answer you receive. Ask them any question you have, and *feel* the answer coming to you. You might hear the answer, or you might see the answer. When you are going into this state of trust and when your angels are giving you the answer, it is important that you respect and honor the answer you are getting. No "What if ..." and no "But ..." Just feel the answer, and feel it fully.

8. Feel your angels touch you and surround you and give you the love and life that is yours. Spend some time relaxing with them, having them explain to you what you want to know. Don't worry about what you will remember. Just trust in the experience.

9. When you feel you have received all you need, allow yourself to slowly come back through the stars, through the clouds, past the trees, back to your sacred place.

10. Become conscious of your breathing. Start to feel yourself back in your body. Take a few moments to reorient yourself, then get paper and pen or your journal, if you keep one. Write down your question, then allow yourself to experience the answer one more time. This is a time to put your conscious self aside and just allow the answer to come through. Write what comes to you, then let it be. Sometimes the questions you ask need a gestation period, a period of incubation, so the answers can reach their full potential. Six weeks or so after you do this meditation, return to your written question and its answer and see how they resonate with you then.

Your angels are with you to help you, to guide you through the lessons of your lifepath. Trust in the information they provide you, and trust in your angels.

Chapter 2

Looking for Your Angels

Who are those beloved beings who care enough about you to touch your life throughout times of stress, turmoil, and chaos, and who continue to love you in quiet times as well? Often they are your loved ones, here on the earth plane as well as on the higher side—and sometimes continuing their work from one area to the other. Most of us are not aware of the subtle influences that touch our lives and help us grow and change. But when we start to closely look at the events and times preceding a major change or growth spurt in our lives, we can begin to notice the angels who come in and touch us.

Loved ones who are in spirit often serve as angels, watching over family members and friends who remain on the earth plane. They may bring messages of assistance, as did my grandfather I never knew, a Talmudic scholar who was born in the late 1870s and passed in the early 1940s, who gave me the answer to a question that stumped me when I was taking my Certified Medium examination. My mother had recently given me a photograph of him—the only photograph of him known to exist—and as I was driving to take the exam, I was extremely nervous. I decided to call upon him and said to him, "Okay, I know we just met, but if you were ever going to help me, help me now!"

I no longer remember the question on the exam, but I clearly recall the answer that came to me as distinctly as if it had been spoken aloud: "Thomas Grinshaw." Although I had never heard my grandfather's voice, I knew immediately that the words had come from him. It was, of course, the right answer. (Is it cheating for a medium to receive exam answers from those on the higher side? There's an interesting question!)

Light Works: Make an Angel Window

Crystals attract, contain, and focus energy. Faceted crystals—those cut with many sides—are especially popular. You can hang small faceted crystals, using string or suction cup hooks, from a window to create your own angel window. As light comes through the window, the crystals refract it into rainbows of color. The colors raise the vibration of the room and add each color's healing properties. Reds, for example, bring energy. Pinks add love. Greens bring peace and harmony. Yellows foster creativity. Enjoy the changing colors as the light varies throughout the day.

Angels Who Watch Over You

Many people tell me of their experiences with angels who save them from injury or in some way pull them from harm's way. My first public demonstration of this as a spirit artist came when a mutual friend asked me to participate in a fund-raising event for someone well known in the psychic community who had been seriously injured in an automobile accident.

I did a reading and spirit drawing for this woman, whom I had not met before that time. During the reading, I saw the angels lift her from her body at the moment of impact in the crash and then return her. When I told her this, she started to cry; it was exactly what she felt had happened. The drawing I did for her was of an angelic form—one of the few times I've drawn angels for people. Although her injuries were severe, she did survive, and today she is completely healed.

But the story doesn't end there. The angels helped this woman in her accident, and the angels brought me to her fund-raiser. My appearance at this event launched my career as a spirit artist.

The concept of divine beings who watch over us enchants and comforts us. It's a wonderful thing to feel that someone is out there, someone who knows more, someone who can guide you through challenging times, someone whose "job" it is to keep you safe.

From ancient civilizations to modern times, people have held some concept of a guardian spirit or guardian angel. Early civilizations such as the Mesopotamians, who lived in the fertile farming valley along the Tigris River, believed that certain of the many gods who ruled their vision of the Universe were the guides and guardians for an individual. The ancient Romans and Greeks similarly connected themselves with certain gods and goddesses or with mythological figures that functioned as messengers of their deities. In early African civilizations, the goddess Oya carried spirits between the higher side and the earth plane at the times of their transitions, birth, and death. In many Native American traditions, guardian spirits often take the form of animals. Christianity, Judaism, and Islam all have adopted the existence of angels as messengers of the divine, establishing systems of classification and categorization with guardian angels uniquely close to God. Within such systems, guardian angels convey prayers to God and messages from God as well as protect individuals from temptation and harm.

I do not believe in such separations and the levels of angels. I believe we are all one and we participate in this beautifully choreographed dance we agreed to before we came to the earth plane. The need to categorize, to separate, has gotten us humans in so much trouble. I view guardian angels in a broad context. Your guardian angel is the divine messenger who chooses who and what guides will work with you, who and what guides have access to you. Your guardian angel might guide a living person to help you such as a brother, a teacher, an aunt, or a neighbor who seems to appear at all the right times to keep you out of harm's way. Sometimes a guardian angel is an unknown being, a spirit guide who oversees your well-being.

I once did a reading for Deb Romaine, who's writing this book with me, in which I described her Native American spirit guide, Featherdancer. Deb is an avid bicyclist who, at the time, was training for a major cycling event. A few weeks after the reading, she was out on a training ride. As she approached an intersection where she had the right-of-way and the cross traffic had a stop sign, she saw that the car coming was going to blow the stop sign. Knowing she could not stop in time or maneuver to avoid a crash, Deb consciously focused her mind on how to best position herself for minimal injury. As both she and the car entered the intersection, the driver made eye contact with Deb but panicked and kept coming. Deb knew she was going to hit the car. Just as the front wheel of Deb's bike was about to make contact with the car, she felt Featherdancer wrap around her like a blanket of energy. She stayed upright on her bike, the car came to a stop, and her bike's front wheel gently bumped the car's front wheel. There was no crash.

Deb's spirit angel, Featherdancer.

Often, a loved one who is in spirit watches over a particular person on the earth plane in a guardian angel way, sometimes through unexpected connections. Thirteen-year-old Rachel knew an angel walked with her. Because she could feel its presence, she wanted to meet this being. Her godmother brought her to see me for a reading and spirit drawing, she herself curious to see who was taking such good care of her goddaughter. The spirit quickly appeared to me and gave me much information about Rachel, who delightedly confirmed every bit of it. I was able to draw Rachel's spirit guardian just as quickly. Although Rachel was pleased to see her guardian angel, to her disappointment, she did not recognize the woman in the drawing. But Rachel's godmother did, and she gasped.

"Did you just draw that?" I nodded. "It's my daughter!" she exclaimed, and her eyes filled with tears as she hugged me. It was her daughter, who had passed to spirit shortly after Rachel's birth and was now watching over Rachel from the higher side just as her mother watched over Rachel on the earth plane.

Your Safety Is Your Responsibility

The one danger a guardian angel cannot save you from is harm you create yourself or expose yourself to through your risk-causing actions. You are responsible for your own safekeeping; your guardian angel is here to help you with doing so but is not going to do it for you. This is the function of free will—*you* make the choices and decisions that direct the unfolding of your lifepath. Some actions incur risk, of course, and sometimes danger is unavoidable. Police officers, firefighters, paramedics, and other emergency response personnel routinely expose themselves to danger in the line of duty; their angels are with them to help protect them and keep them safe. You might find yourself caught driving in an unexpected downpour or snowstorm. If you do, ask your angels to help you drive carefully, focus on the road conditions, and arrive safely at your destination.

Light Works: Chapter 2 Angel Card

This chapter's angel card word is *Divine*. The divine is the energy that connects us all. What does it mean to receive from the higher realms? Stop for a moment and go into the quiet. Think of the colors and movement that will inspire you, then create your second angel card, *Divine*.

Staying on Track

Spirit, the essence of the higher being, sometimes requires physicality—a physical body that exists in a physical environment—to complete some of its lessons. So we come to the earth plane, we incarnate, to follow the lifepath that will take us through these lessons. We will face difficulties, things we have to overcome, things we have to let go of, in day-to-day life. This is part of our evolutionary process, our soul growth. It is also part of the evolutionary process for those who remain on the higher side to help us complete our work here on the earth plane. To stay on track, we are asked to trust in our connections with the higher beings so we can put our energy where it's supposed to be.

Sometimes we see people who have been given what looks like an incredible gift, but it's not what they're intended to be doing. Other times we can see people who appear to have incredible gifts they're not using. But we never know a person's lifepath, and things are not always as they appear. Sometimes what feels like the wrong path is simply paving the way for another. My own life is a good example of this.

I studied art, then religion, then psychology—and now I combine all three in my work as a spirit artist. But this is not the path I saw myself traveling when I first embarked on it. I thought my life was going to be about being a painter. I was doing well with my painting, but my career just wasn't falling into place in quite the ways I thought it should be. I was getting some shows but not the big ones. I was selling some of my work but not as much as I wanted.

Interested in religion, I studied it and became a Spiritualist minister. But I kept painting because that was really what I wanted to do and *all* I really wanted to do. On December 31, 1996, my husband came home and said he had a new perk at work—tuition reimbursement for spouses. Now I could go to graduate school. Everyone who knew me and my love of art thought I'd go back to school for art, but when I meditated on it, I got the message, clear and strong, to study psychology. So that's what I did. I earned my Master of Science degree in psychological counseling, and for a period of time in my life I worked as a counselor while I continued to paint and do spirit readings.

When a woman I met found out I did spirit readings, she told me she was an astrologer and asked if I wanted to exchange readings. If I would do a spirit reading for her, she would do an astrology reading for me. During her astrology reading for me, she said, "You're an artist. Are you a sculptor? Your work is so big!" I said no, I was a painter. She looked at me and said, "You are working in state institutions, and if you continue, you will be sick."

In fact I was working as a counselor in a state institution at the time, and I'd been feeling I needed to make a change. I loved my work, but it was grueling and the conditions were difficult. The astrologer's reading affirmed my sense that now was the time to make a change. When I went to my counseling job the next day, I gave my three-weeks notice. Then I asked my angels and spirit guides what to do and determined I would trust the answer the Universe gave me. I sent out resumés for counseling positions and at the same time started calling all the places

I'd done readings in the past. I got one interview as a result of my resumé, but I did not get the job, which was the first time ever in my life I had not gotten a job following an interview. But within two weeks, I had filled up three months' worth of readings. I got my answer from the Universe, and it put me back on track for my lifepath.

Do your life lessons feel unfairly harsh? Ask yourself whether or not you're gaining from the struggles. Life is not supposed to be easy. People tend to believe that if they're following their paths then everything should be easy. But we're always learning and being tested, and that is not easy. If you get it, you can look at it and recognize the lesson and then let go. We've agreed to the path we're on. The lessons we're going to learn sometimes require people to come into our lives and touch us in ways that are uncomfortable because that's what it takes for us to learn the lesson. We have to let go of our ego so we can let the circumstance be what it is, learn the lesson, and move on.

In the Light: Correcting Your Course

"I'm about to make an important change in my life. Is it the right one?" So many people come to me with this question. The answer to these questions is not always obvious or what you expect; it is within you, though, if you search for it and open yourself to receiving it. Sometimes we feel driven to make changes that don't seem to make sense, or we might try to stay in circumstances we want to be "right" but in our heart of hearts we know are not. Ask your angels to guide you, to come look at the situation with you, and to help you find the solutions that will keep you on or return you to your lifepath.

Take a look at what changes you are about to make. Write them down so you have clarity around your expression of them:

_____

_____

_____

Go to your sacred space, if you've created one, or just to a location where you can be undisturbed. Go into a meditative state, and ask your guides and angels to come look at the situation with you. Explore the alternatives available to you. Let your angels and guides lead you along the paths of each; often there are numerous paths that will take you to the same place. Write three possibilities:

_____

_____

_____

Ask your angels and guides, "What do you think of each of these alternatives?" What responses do you receive? Write them down:

_____

_____

_____

How does each response feel to you? Try it on; experience it through your meditation. If you feel the voice in your head is answering, trust in the response.

Angels as Agents of Change

I became comfortably settled in my work as a spirit artist. I had a small but steady stream of clients, and I loved what I was doing. Then one day Bob Olson, developer and editor of the website and online magazine OfSpirit.com, changed my life. Bob saw my portfolio and wanted to interview me about my work and do an article about me on the website. As a result of this article, my public profile and my business took a giant leap. I sometimes joke that Bob Olson is my business guardian angel and that he is here to lift me up and help me fly. I look at it as the way we touch each other, illuminate each other, and bring light to each other, as we follow the path we are here on Earth to do.

Do you have such angels working in your life? Who are some of the people, the earth angels, who have given (or opened you) to opportunities and possibilities? Take a few moments to consider them and their influences as you answer these questions:

1. Think of a time in your life when you knew you needed to change but you resisted or were reluctant. This might have involved a job or career, a relationship, or a residence. What nudged (or shoved!) you into action?

2. Now, think about the events and circumstances that precipitated that change. Were there people in your life who touched you, encouraged you, or even goaded or pushed you in the direction of the change?

3. If you can't recall such a person, can you remember if there was a familiar feeling whenever the circumstances were present, perhaps the smell of a fragrance or a song that, either at the time of the experience or now as you are recalling it, reminded you of someone who has passed?

4. Let this recollection simmer in your thoughts for a few minutes. Then write a paragraph or two, on a piece of paper or in your journal, that describes the circumstances and events preceding the change and how the change came about.

Do you get a sense of angelic intervention as you contemplate these questions and the events in your life they evoke? It is sometimes surprising to identify those who act as angels in our lives. Even people who present us with challenge and difficulty can function as angels when they motivate us to grow and evolve.

> What a piece of work is a man! How noble in reason! How infinite in faculty! In form, in moving, how express and admirable! In action how like an angel! In apprehension how like a god!
> —William Shakespeare (1564–1616), playwright, *Hamlet*, Act II

In the Light: Ask for Archangel Michael's Help

In Jewish, Christian, and Islamic tradition, the archangel Michael represents the courage and ability to make change. Think of what rules and regulations you have set in your life that are holding you back. The essence of Archangel Michael can help you change.

Write down a rule or pattern you feel is holding you back:

_____

_____

_____

Archangel Michael is always seen holding a sword. Ask him to pass that sword to you so you can cut through the old patterns of your past. List the patterns you would like to see changed:

_____

_____

_____

Visualize yourself holding the sword and cutting through the old rules or patterns and setting them free to go out to the ethos for the highest and the best.

Ask for the right outcome to occur and see it as done:

_____

_____

_____

Those Who Challenge and Test You

It's important to remember that your path in life is one of learning that leads to personal growth. The lessons are not always easy, even when you're following your path. Sometimes people have to come into your life and touch you in ways that are uncomfortable, because that's what it takes for you to learn your lessons. Caroline Myss, author of several books including the best-selling *Sacred Contracts: Awakening Your Divine Potential* (Harmony Books, 2002), observes that if your lifepath's purpose is for you to learn unconditional love, then someone is going to hurt or disappoint you, because that's how you learn to love someone unconditionally.

The angels in our lives support us as we learn and remind us that through our lessons we grow and evolve—even (or perhaps especially) those angels who challenge and test us. I look at some of the people in my life who have hurt me the most, and I call them my angels because they have helped—and sometimes forced—me to grow and change.

When Angels Seem to Fail You

You may have felt the anguish of personal loss or struggle and wonder where your angels were *then?* Where were the angels when I, or my loved one, needed them most? Why did they not rush to the rescue and stop that heart attack or divert that drunk driver? Such loss is very difficult to bear and sometimes tests the capacity of faith beyond what seems reasonable. But what we cannot see are the varied situations and perhaps widespread outcomes that evolve as a result of this loss we feel so personally and so deeply. Sometimes great good, individual and collective, comes from the changes imposed by great loss.

"I asked for help. Why didn't I get it?" I often hear this question from people who are struggling to cope with or understand setbacks and losses in their lives. Father Rizzo, a Roman Catholic priest, had the best response I've ever heard for this question: "God answered your prayer; he just said no." Sometimes we don't get what we ask for, what we want right now, because it's not for our *highest and best*. We do receive, however, the help we need to guide the unfolding of our lifepaths.

There are those who say the Universe is in chaos; others say it is the divine order of things that good and bad coexist. As human beings, we have an incomplete view of the Universe. Our experiences, as individuals and as members of the world community, define what we know and shape our view. There is much, much more that we *don't* know. We don't know the ramifications, for the immediate or for the long-term future, of events and happenings. We don't know the path of the ripples; we only see the stone skip on the surface and enter the water.

Loss is often mundane, although it might have a far-reaching effect on your life. Perhaps a cascade of miscues and delays causes you to watch your connecting flight take off without you, leaving you stranded at the airport. *(The stone.)* But maybe you end up sharing a table in the airline's lounge with the HR director of a company recruiting for a job that exactly matches your interests and qualifications. Or maybe you find yourself standing in line at the coffee kiosk with the dean of admissions for the college you're considering and learn that six new scholarships just became available in your field of study. *(The ripples.)* And 30 years from now—an impossible distance in time now, perhaps, but that will soon enough seem short—your architecture or painting or writing or invention redefines the standard. *(More ripples.)* These things can—and do—happen.

There are two ways of spreading light: to be the candle or the mirror that reflects it.
—Edith Wharton (1862–1937), American author

In the Light: You, Too, Are an Angel

The Spiritualist viewpoint is that angels are the ones who give you messages, help, and healing. Are you any less of an angel than someone on the higher realm for what you're doing or what you've done for others? Just as others are angels in our lives—friends, family members, co-workers, even complete strangers who happen along at opportune moments—we are angels in the lives of others. Did you ever ...

- Trade seats on a cross-country flight so members of a family could sit together?

- Offer a handful of change to the person in front of you in the grocery store checkout line who came up a little bit short for paying the bill?

- Take a walk with your partner or child even though you had other plans for using your time?

- Push the elevator button for someone whose hands were full, then ride to that floor to hold the door?

- Stop your car to let a family of raccoons, deer, or ducks safely cross the road?

- Stay after work to help a colleague finish a report or prepare for a meeting?

- Withhold the certain-to-be-hurtful words that rushed to the tip of your tongue in an argument?

You do countless good deeds for others each day. Many of your actions are simply the behaviors that define you. If you are a health-care provider, firefighter, police officer, or teacher, for example, helping others will be part of your job. No matter what you spend your days doing, you are an angel in the lives of others. Here is a brief exercise to help you identify the ways in which your angel-self emerges.

Take three deep, cleansing breaths to clear your thoughts and calm your mind. Now, take a look at all you do, directly and indirectly, for so many others in your life. After you've answered these questions, send a message to your unconscious about what a special person you are!

1. List as many good things about you as you can think of:

   _____

   _____

   _____

2. Write down three ways in which you've given of your time, energy, or material possessions for the benefit of someone else this week. Don't be afraid to think small! Did you help someone reach an

item on a higher shelf at the market? Take the time to talk to someone who was lonely or afraid? Give a donation?

_____

_____

_____

3. To whom did you send loving thoughts, healing energy, or prayers?

_____

_____

_____

4. List three ways you might be able to help others more than you already do:

_____

_____

_____

5. Set an intention for what you hope to accomplish this week that might be helpful to others:

_____

_____

_____

Highest and Best: Meet Your Inner Angel

Some people believe that an angel is one whose spirit is so pure that he or she did not have to walk the earth plane. Each of us has that purity within us. This meditation will show you how to see that beautiful pure self, that angel within you:

1. Find a place to sit that is quiet and where you will not be interrupted. You might sit in your sacred space, near the water, or in any quiet place that is yours alone. Turn off the phone and tell family members or friends you are taking some time for yourself. You might want to record this meditation first and follow its guidance as you go to meet your inner angel.

2. Begin by taking three deep breaths, in through your nose and out through your mouth. Take a deep breath in through your nose to clear your body, then release it. Take a second breath to open your mind and a third to free your spirit.

3. Visualize yourself walking into a beautiful home. Visualize this home as you always imagined the most wonderful home you could imagine would be. See yourself walking into the home and walking up to a mirror.

4. Visualize, in this mirror, your physical self, the self you show to the outside world. See how you appear to others. Spend a few moments with this physical self and enjoy him or her, then release the image.

5. Now visualize your emotional self. How do you feel inside, and how does that look? Make no judgments here, just see it. Smooth any ruffled places. Send them healing, and work with them until the sharp edges dissipate. Breathe in the relaxed feeling, stay with that feeling for a while, then release it.

6. Continue looking in that mirror and visualize your spiritual self. This is the pure spirit that lives within each of us. See that pure spirit, the love and light that emanates from your spirit. See the colors and the luminescence. Stay with that image and appreciate the beauty that freely flows from you. *You are an angel.*

Chapter 3

What an Angel Has to Tell You About Life and Love

In writing this book on how you can empower your life with angels, I decided to do something adventurous, perhaps even a bit controversial, as we complete the first part of our empowering angel work together. In Chapter 1, we explored the many ideas people have about angels and why we human beings believe in their ethereal light—across cultures and even civilizations, borders, boundaries, and time. In Chapter 2, we investigated the process of where and how we look for the angels in our lives. In later chapters, we'll take our work deeper, and I'll give you focused exercises that will connect you to your angels, help you communicate with them by both sending and receiving messages, and help you recognize your own angelic essence. Rung by rung, you'll learn how to climb Jacob's biblical ladder as you grow closer and closer to a conscious awareness of how angels empower your existence every day. Now though, here in this third chapter, before we go any farther, let's leave the climb up Jacob's ladder as an exercise for another day and take the express elevator straight to the penthouse. In other words, let's dare to reach straight up to the Divine. *Let's go directly to the higher realm and talk to an angel.*

In my work as a Spiritualist minister and psychic medium, I sometimes, but not often, go into trance to make contact with beings of Spirit, both loved ones who have passed on and also spirit guides and angelic beings. The trance state is a very deep and intimate zone of altered consciousness that takes much preparation and training to enter. As I began to work through the content for this book, looking toward the optimal way to share with you the process of developing a relationship with your angels and spirit guides, I came to the discovery, an epiphany of sorts, that the *best* way to show you that you *can* speak to your angels and guides would be to use my gift to do just that. By sitting in on and participating in this focused angel communication session with me, my co-author Deb Romaine, and our book producer at Amaranth, Lee Ann Chearney, you will become a part of this special exchange of questions and answers with an angelic being. More than a witness, you will share in this Divine experience with us. We've saved a chair for you, dear reader: for the message of this angel is *meant* for *you*, so you will believe, and so you will be given the courage to continue and persevere with the all-important work that lies ahead for you.

Your climb up Jacob's Ladder to commune with your angels and guides might seem sometimes an arduous rung-by-rung affair, and sometimes an effortless joyful glide. Let me reassure you that it makes no difference which impression of the path you encounter—arduous or effortless; both are valid and equally rewarding. What is essential is the effort to continue reaching up, growing, learning, and exploring. In this book you won't learn how to enter a trance state—that level of connection with the higher realm can take many years to achieve—but you will find out how to use meditation and other techniques to connect to the Divine flow of energy that is all around you and so access the angels and spirits that accompany you on your human journey. And as you work with your angels, understand that your soul is agreeing to do angelic work! When you empower your life with angels, you become one with the Divine harmony and as such, become an instrument of good, of peace, and of healing. Whether you feel and perceive your actions and daily routine of living as full of wonder or simply as mundane happenings, they will become infused with Divine purpose and potential.

We have glimpsed something greater, something of liberating power, and there are no external obstructions to our movement out of limitation and into that freedom.

—Sister Wendy Beckett (1930–), art historian

Rising

Entering trance is an intense physical, emotional, and spiritual endeavor, one that asks for all of you, for everything. What you'll read here is the record and result of two trance sessions I did with Deb and Lee Ann over the course of a weekend. In fact, it was the first weekend of the new year 2004—a good time to be consulting the higher realm, a time of new beginnings! As you read the words and receive the message of an angelic being unfolding in the pages to come, I'll also share with you the visuals of, emotions about, and insights on what I sensed and saw during trance.

To prepare for entering the trance state, I sat in quiet meditation alone for about 15 minutes. I often use a chart of the many symbols and names for God as a point of focus for connecting to the Source during this time. When I felt ready, properly centered and grounded, I came into the room where I would hold the angel communication session and joined Deb and Lee Ann, who were ready both to ask questions and to record the messages given. Sitting comfortably in meditative pose, I closed my eyes and began to rise. As I ascended, I asked for contact with the higher realm:

Divine Source, lead me to the spirit guide for this book, Empowering Your Life with Angels.

It is interesting; I remember when I was going up—each time I go into trance this way it is a new experience, so I can't say this is what happens every time—I first saw somebody who seemed quite priestly. I asked, "Are you the one?" and kept going, up, up, up. We had set the intent at the start of the session, that's what I was doing as I entered the prayer state, and I continued to pass upward, guided through layers of spirit, always asking the question, "Are you the one? Are you the one? Are you the one?" as I passed ever higher. It felt like it wasn't yet what we needed. So still I kept going up until all of a sudden I connected with a spirit who agreed to speak for this book. It felt as if I had been led to her and she to me, a very nice coming together.

Light Works: Chapter 3 Angel Card

This chapter's angel card word is *Guidance*. Your angels and spirit guides are here, with you now, to provide guidance and assistance. All you have to do is ask them to help you. When you hold your *Guidance* angel card in your hands and look at the design you've created, you should feel open and receptive to the energy and the wisdom of the Divine and of the Universe. Use shapes, colors, and images to craft your *Guidance* angel card.

There I Am Elucia

Until this moment of coming together, Deb and Lee Ann tell me that I looked very much like a searching Rita! But in that instant of awareness and greeting, my expression—this is what they told me—became quite serene, benevolently amused, much like the smile of the *Mona Lisa*. In trance, I saw the spirit; she showed me her form. But the rest of the time, during which she spoke, it was not like that. The rest of the time I saw through *her* eyes and spoke her words. What a rush of sensory details I experienced in that moment of coming together as "Rita" stepped aside! As her essence in spirit made contact with my human form, she began to express with obvious joy the delight of each blade of grass, the textures, the smells, the rising evening star—all the contrasts inherent in human perception. She took me, Rita, on a tour of Port Townsend, the Pacific Northwest town where Deb, Lee Ann, and I were located (on an Earth map ...) for these trance sessions. And of course, the first questions came:

Are you an angel? Yes, as you would describe and understand such a being.

Where do you come from? It is not a tangible place. When I am there, I am merged. We all come together as a community, as one. We are complete.

The visual shifted, and I felt myself moving beyond the planets. Yet in the same place, the visuals that were coming in were of incredible colors. At one form we paused and I remember seeing something that, paradoxically, seemed almost a feeling of what you would imagine it looks like underwater but you are not underwater. Often in trance the senses blur and you can feel sights, see touch, and hear taste. A piece of light spiraled from the whole, expressing a need to go to the earth, not like something broken, but like something *given. We're going to give this piece so they can come and they can receive and then we'll take it back.* That was the energy. And it was so gentle, so soft that it was not of anything I could say was something that would have to be feared. In trance, I knew she had led me to her soul group, the Divine whole from which she had emerged to speak with us.

Do you lose yourself? No. How do you know? Old memories.
Do you welcome the merging? Oh, yes! We are not afraid. There is nothing to be afraid of. There is no fear.

*What is your name? On Earth, I was Dianna. **Is Dianna your name now?** There I Am Elucia.*

Dianna went on to describe her incarnation on the earth plane. She had lived in ancient Greece, the mother of three children. One of the children, a daughter, remained with her always while the other two children had gone on to do their own work. Dianna mused quite affectionately of a son who dwelled with the horses in an ethereal place, not a physical place. She identified Elucia as the name of her soul group and explained that Dianna had traveled to us as in the human form sent to speak.

After the first trance session, Deb, Lee Ann, and I headed straight to the *Oxford Companion to Classical Literature*. Who had we been speaking to? Our first impulse was to look up the moon goddess Diana, but this seemed too easy—and somehow, just too incredible! We decided to look deeper, and our search led us to Eileithyia, the Greek goddess of childbirth, identified with Hera (the Roman goddess Juno), mother of Mars, the god of war. Mars, traditionally, is a great lover of horse racing. So did the Divine guide me in trance to a soul group of ancient power and wisdom? Perhaps.

What we do know is that Dianna/Elucia's maternal bearing and enduring message of the need for peace, inner reflection, and compassion in the midst of human conflict and troubled times on the earth plane is consistent with Eileithyia's place and purpose in her ancient pantheon as a guardian of birth, new life, and sacred possibility. In that Jungian way of embracing the shadow side (psychoanalyst Carl Jung, trained by Sigmund Freud, believed that humanity expresses itself in balancing archetypes, such as light and shadow), Eileithyia professes deep and abiding love for her son, a war-maker, while advocating that all human experience leads ultimately, inexorably, to peace, to the Divine. You'll discover just what we mean as we continue to reveal Dianna/Elucia's angelic message—the message of her soul group—for you, and for the highest and best in us all.

Elucia's Messages About Life

Also during the first trance session, Elucia spoke repeatedly about the need for human beings to overcome their fears and suffering, both individually and collectively, and of a return, *always*, to the center of the

Eternal Divine: *We come here to Earth not just to struggle. We come here to learn to embrace ourselves, to know that* this *is what we are part of.* The visual coming in at this time for me in trance was so gorgeous, the colors so profound and rich, full of beautiful, awesome, and inspiring light. I am an artist, and I can tell you there is no earthly visual image that could give true justice to this vision of Divine paradise. Even the spectacular images of the *Hubble* space telescope pale in comparison. We can take encouragement and comfort from Elucia's message and the gift of her vision.

What can we do to reclaim our spiritual connection to the Divine? Ask for it.

When you are in human form, can you touch the Divine? Yes, but it is not easy.

She goes on to tell us: *The true essence of each of us is craving to learn soul lessons, but on the earth plane we don't often know or recognize this truth—and this is where the fear comes from. But there is no obstacle that cannot be overcome.* The human experience, it would seem, as elucidated by Elucia, is a process of relearning, returning. *You wonder,* Elucia continues, *but you know. A droplet of color placed in a glass of water doesn't disappear; it just encompasses All. You change the color of the water just as your being here changes the earth.* In this simple image, Elucia reminds us of the importance of each individual human life and its unique contribution to the Divine Whole. She has catapulted us full circle from a contemplation of a visual of the Divine beyond human comprehension to one that resonates on an earthly plane of human understanding.

In the second trance session, we wanted to ask Elucia more about our human form, our earthly mission, and what it means to be Divinely human.

In the Light: Layers of Being

I recall I had been somewhat reluctant to go into trance again for a second session with Dianna/Elucia. We'd been working with such concentration on the book during my trip from Boston to Port Townsend. I'd been leading Deb and Lee Ann in connecting to Spirit for several days continuously and, as you can easily imagine, going back and forth from the angelic realm is demanding and can put some wear and tear on mere mortals. All three of us, though, were eager to receive more knowledge from the Elucia soul group, and to accomplish this, I knew connecting through trance was my only alternative. And so once again I entered a deep trance state and ascended to find Dianna/Elucia waiting, content, as if patiently anticipating my return and our questions.

So once again Elucia spoke through me as Dianna. As I allowed her spirit to use my body to communicate, I felt my throat chakra activate, and as the words began to come, my heart chakra and my third eye chakra filled with light. It was as if a huge funnel of cosmic energy entered my head through the thousand-petalled lotus chakra at its crown, moving in and then lifting up, supporting and at the same time, leading. It was an unusual experience, definitely an unusual experience. But that's what it felt like—that moment of greeting and connection.

Welcome Elucia. *Thank you. Thank you for inviting me back. You've been very busy.*

We want to give advice to our readers to help them connect to Spirit. How can we as humans ... what can we do for Spirit? *The process we're trying to create is that of helping each person become attached to who he or she is. When we learn to take the time, to peel away each of the layers, we will learn to understand, seeing that each one is like a fruit that is ready to come to fruition. Each one has to open and peel away the outer garb.*

How do we do that? *We ask Spirit to connect with you as you ask to connect to Spirit. You ask to come together. You ask that one piece, one layer at a time be peeled away from the outer surface. We ask that one at a time we open up and allow the true essence to boldly come through. We ask that one layer at a time be peeled away gently. Take it, put it to the side and acknowledge each new layer as if it's a new being.*

Each layer of what? *We come with an outer skin when we come to the earth plane. We come with this outer skin of protection we feel we have to guard. As we take off each layer, as we move each layer off, it allows the true essence of the human, their True Spirit, to come through.*

So we become more as you, as Spirit? *You will still maintain your physical body, but you will become truer to the essence of who you are. It's* *like the unfoldment of the flower. When you watch a rose bloom, first the bud opens and you watch that peel back, then each petal opens until eventually you get to the center and the full fragrance comes through. Each petal, as it opens on the being, has to gently be removed and laid aside, lovingly, caringly so the next layer can open.*

Elucia's message about shedding layers to reveal our most essential being no doubt has personal meaning for each person who attempts to understand and interpret it. Perhaps the layers are the many layers of the subtle body, from physical to astral, if you believe these layers exist. Perhaps the layers are our many incarnations as we return again and again, reincarnated to the earth plane, each time with the soft skin of a newborn child, ready and eager to learn and to absorb knowledge; many people believe this is possible. Perhaps the layers are the armor of our experiences in this life, put up with the intent to shield and protect us, but which ultimately only block the Divine light of our true selves from free expression. However you perceive the layers described by Elucia, the process of unfoldment she describes is very important in doing your work with your spirit guides and your angels. To reach to the Divine, you must make yourself accessible.

So how accessible *are* you, right now as you read this? How many layers do you have? Are they tough and resistant or pliant and yielding? Wherever you are, find a spot to sit alone for several minutes in quiet meditation on the visual of your layers held tightly about you as a bud not yet ready to risk bursting into blossom. Place your hands on each elbow and hug them close to your body as you breathe deeply and feel your breath move inward to the center of your protected being. Hold your breath for as long as you feel comfortable. Now, as you release your breath, extend your hands in front of you, palms up and fingers spread. Breathe in again, and move your wrists to touch, forming the protected shape of an open blossom with your cupped palms and spread fingers. Place your hands before your throat chakra and allow this open blossom to gently hold and support your life force energy as you continue to breathe in and out. See this breath as Divine energy moving into and out of your body, much as I felt Elucia's energy fill me as I entered trance, and with each inhale and exhale imagine, *feel,* the layers melt away as the Divine enters and surrounds you. Speak the Sanskrit word *Om,* if you like, the primal sound of the Universe.

Light Works: It Begins by Asking

What if the layers will not yield? *If you look at this as an adventure, the adventure of opening up to the being you were meant to be ...*

And it begins by asking? *And it begins by asking.*

What do we ask? *You ask Infinite Spirit, God, the Divine, the Light, the essence of which we come, to help. You ask for protection. You ask that with each new ... each new period of time, each day, each hour, each minute, each layer, that as it comes off it be acknowledged and laid to rest so you can come to the next piece. Each one is a new time, and that piece of unfoldment is what you are creating. As you open it up, as you look at it, as you experience each part of your life, permit yourself to bless it. Bless it. Look at it as this: what is its purpose in my life? The guides will answer you, the angels will answer you, the answers come from the Divine for the level of acceptance you have at the time. Allow this to happen, let go of the fight, although for some the fight is necessary but for others it is not.*

I can't think of much that I would add to these words from Elucia. Remember them and use them to guide and comfort you as we continue our work together in future chapters of this book. They can help you empower your life with angelic energy and Divine wisdom. When something is too difficult, ask for help, ask for blessing—for *every* experience. Know that what happens to each of us in our lives, moment to moment, day to day, is a part of our path, our journey to the Divine. Every experience is valuable. And when you become more accessible, you will learn how to allow your angels to show you what this means (it is not just a cliché!), as you learn to allow your guides in spirit to help you peel away the layers to reveal your highest and best self.

A human being is a part of the whole called by us "the universe," a part limited in time and space. He experiences himself, his thoughts and feelings, as something separate from the rest—a kind of optical delusion of consciousness. This delusion is a kind of prison for us, restricting us to our personal desires and affection for a few persons nearest to us. Our task must be to free ourselves from this prison by widening the circle of understanding and compassion to embrace all living creatures and the whole of nature in its beauty.

—Albert Einstein (1879–1955), physicist and writer

Elucia's Messages About Love

We'd asked Elucia about our own essential natures, and now we wanted to ask what we could do for ourselves—and for others.

What can we do in these uncertain times; how can we make the world a better place? A question we've been trying to answer since the beginning of time …. The times truly are troubled. There is great difficulty in the world right now. Many people have chosen before they've come here to sacrifice themselves for the betterment of others. There are people who have chosen to come through war or natural devastation for us to look for those people living in the affluent societies who are not struck by the devastation.

It is their job to let go of themselves and their own ego for even a short time each day and to send the healing to the home. To look and see … the newspapers are such … filled with print, words, words, words, more words, yet saying very little … There is fear existing even in this country where people are living in total comfort. If we look, if we take the time to connect with Spirit and ask that the light and the healing be sent … We need to understand how powerful thought is, we need to understand how powerful and creative we are, even the people here on the earth plane who think of themselves as so powerless, the power of their thought is so great. Some will do it in physical, some will do it in affirmation, and some will do it in prayer. But if we take the pieces, we can put it together to send that healing energy to surround the earth—the earth is very small, you know.

I remember a friend coming to me once to tell me about a discussion she had with an office colleague about a difficult situation at her work. At one point in the meeting, she told me, "Rita, my colleague called me naive and actually asked me how many people get up in the morning and *really* look for ways during the day to make the world a better place?" "I do," she told her colleague, undeterred. "And lots of other people do, too!" Bravo. In accepting our work with the angels, Elucia guides, we must not only become accessible, we must also become *available*.

In the Light: The Eye of the Beholder

What do you find most beautiful about humanity? Its innocence.

What do you find most beautiful about Spirit? Its vastness. It goes on forever.

Elucia has given her answers. What are yours?
What do you find most beautiful about humanity?

_____

_____

What do you find most beautiful about Spirit?

_____

_____

_____

Coming Together in Love and Light

What happens when humanity and Spirit connect at their optimal point? The connection between Earth, or the earth ones, and spirit ... When we connect all is healed, all is healed. We keep looking for the way when the way is obvious. We keep looking for a way separate from what we know to be the truth, and yet it comes back as being obvious. The obvious truth is that we are Spirit, even here on the earth plane. And when we are connected, when we trust in that ability, and when we take that energy, we can connect with it from the high realms and spread it out and surround the world with it. That's when all will heal. Each time we are in fear, we make a hole of darkness, and in that hole of darkness we create sores that fester. As we allow ourselves to connect into that beautiful energy of Spirit and spread it and visualize the entire Earth being surrounded with it, we spread more and more healing. You ask how we can heal the earth, how we from the higher side and those of the earth plane can come together. If we take the time to come together, if we take the time to visualize that healing energy being spread upon the entire Earth, if we see that light—see it, see it in your mind, see that healing happens, see it spread, see it encompassed around your planet— that's when healing will happen. The spirit world is desperately trying to get through to those of you on the earth plane to do this work. Do it. Do it.

Earlier in this chapter we wondered whether Elucia could actually be the soul group energy of Eileithyia, mother of the god of war, protectress of women in childbirth. Whether that's true or not true (and believe me, I'd never *heard* of Eileithyia until we found her in the *Oxford Companion* after our first trance session ...), we can see and respect the appropriateness and maturity in Elucia's message that would come only from such a Divine being. Only such a mother could show us the path to love in times when anger and fear seem all-consuming, dividing us from ourselves, from one another, and from the Divine. If you feel you are called by your angels to healing work, embrace this sacred path and walk it with patience and determination. Understand that even though as humans we are not born with angel wings to fly, our steps can lead us to the miraculous, one by one.

Grounding

I had asked Deb and Lee Ann to end the second trance session with Elucia after 20 minutes so I could preserve as much energy for my plane trip back to Boston that afternoon as possible. Our time together, and with Elucia, was coming to a close. Still, we lingered for one more question.

Is there a final message you feel we should know and pass along to our readers on behalf of Spirit or of yourself? What I'm being shown now is a flower and a dove. The flower is beautiful, it's an orchid, I'm not sure of what kind, it's yellow in color. As I see it, and I see it now, I'm being asked to tell you that what you have here is fragile. It needs to be cared for. What you have here is beautiful. What you envision as angels is those wings of a bird and the beauty of the flower that come together as constant reminders of what we are about. Allow yourself to help others, and teach others that we on the higher side are trying to work with you.

I could feel that my physical being needed to reconnect to Rita. Returning from the higher realm to the human body is a challenging experience, never an easy one. If ascending is a weightless movement upward, descending has the opposite effect. Deb and Lee Ann moved quickly to bring me a blanket and a glass of water as I turned pale and shivered into the center of my human being. The shiver isn't from being cold, so much as from the shock of finding myself once again of the body. Returning feels like I am sitting in a concrete block. Everything is so much heavier, blander.

Ironically, my human perception of returning to the body after experiencing the intense visuals and stimulation of the higher realm is the mirror of Elucia's delight in human perception. I suppose the grass *is* always greener on the other side! After relaxing in meditation for about 10 minutes or so, I asked for my sketchbook and art supplies. It was time to draw Dianna/Elucia as she had presented herself to me. And here she is.

Rita's drawing of angelic being Dianna/Elucia.

Angelic Guides: The Committee

Dianna and her soul group Elucia connected with me in trance state for the specific purpose of bringing an angelic message to you through this book. We all, though, as individuals, possess what many mediums call a Committee, which is a Divine spirit collective that guides and nurtures each one of us. This Committee emerges from the Source and serves as our connection to it and as the motivator to direct us toward our higher purpose. Ask in meditation for the name of the guide who speaks to you on behalf of your Committee—remember it is a collective of Spirit.

You Look Like About the Kind of Angel I'd Get ...

When I offered to connect through Spirit to Lee Ann's Committee, to have an example to show to our readers, she readily agreed to allow this to happen. As I've said, each person's Committee emerges from the Divine and is pretty high up there in the spirit realm. However, as an individual's Committee and facilitating guide are here precisely to nurture and shepherd our Divine humanity, they prove easier to find than the angelic being Elucia had been, and so I can connect to them without enduring the rigors of a trance session.

As I put out the intent to communicate with Lee Ann's Committee and facilitating guide, I began to see the spirits who surround her, much as I do with any person for whom I do a spirit reading and drawing. I saw her grandmother Jessie, who had just passed to Spirit, standing with her own mother Vennera (Vennera's spirit drawing appears in Chapter 1). I saw an interesting fellow who looked a bit like ET, but I wasn't sure if Lee Ann was ready to handle this and so I moved on. It was as if spirit after spirit stepped aside until one emerged, surrounded by five others. He identified himself as Lee Ann's facilitating guide, the spokesman for her Committee, and agreed to allow me to draw her Committee for her.

Rita's drawing of Lee Ann's Committee in Spirit.

Now this is a pretty intense group. The facilitating guide communicated that he was the one who connected to Lee Ann's open heart. From our left to right in viewing the drawing, the members of the Committee presented themselves as her guides to pathos and compassion, humor, the task master (he helps Lee Ann, our book producer, get authors to deliver manuscripts on time!), the scientist, and the poet. Lee Ann had her hand over her mouth just about the whole time I made this drawing, but her partner, Tom, came right out and quoted one of her favorite movie lines from *It's a Wonderful Life*, the line where George tells Clarence, "Well, you look like about the kind of angel I'd get ..." My Committee, Tom joked, probably looks more like The Three Stooges. What a fine Committee that would be!

As you work through the exercises in this book and become more and more experienced in connecting to your guides and angels, we encourage you to invite your Committee and your facilitating guide to show their forms to you. Thank your Committee and facilitating guide for their care, and ask their help for your continued unfoldment.

Highest and Best: Reaching for the Source

Remember earlier I said we'd lingered with Elucia for one last question? Well, that was actually the *penultimate* question. Here is the ultimate one.

So we're not alone? You are not alone. You never were. We've always been together. This earth was created by creative thought. Healing is a process of creative thought. Each of us has that ability to create from the higher side, to create from the heart. Tell your people, tell them to open their hearts and allow that energy from the higher side to come through and touch each other with that love. That's how you heal this earth. The bombs are just temporary; the buildings are just temporary; your spirit is Eternal.

We know, dear reader, you will join us in expressing our gratitude to Dianna and the Elucia soul group and to the Source, the ultimate guide of all in spirit and on Earth for her wisdom and blessings:

Namaste. Thank you.

And now, strengthened and nurtured by this message of light and love, and with our personal Committees of Divine guides ready to facilitate on our behalf, let's continue our empowering angel work together.

Part 2

Seeing Your Angels: No One Is Alone Who Has Friends

We all experience times of questioning and challenge. In the 1946 Frank Capra film *It's a Wonderful Life,* now a holiday classic, heaven sends the angel Clarence to show despondent George Bailey the many ways his life has touched and changed the lives of others. Clarence is not what George expects in an angel, but Clarence shows George that angels take many forms. George sees that the true angels in his life are his friends ... and that he has many, many of them.

Like George, often we fail to recognize the angels in our lives. Maybe we're looking for white-robed figures, halos, and wings. Although art through the ages overflows with such images, in truth, angels take many forms. We have to look for them as they are, not as we think they should be. What do your angels look like?

Remember this: No man is a failure who has friends.

—Angel Second Class Clarence (played by Henry Travers) in *It's a Wonderful Life* (1946)

Chapter 4

On Rays of Light:
How Angels Appear

There always have been and there always will be people on the earth plane who are more open to see the possibilities of what the healing energies from the higher side can bring. You can go back to biblical times or 15,000 years and find the seers, soothsayers, and prophets. These people conveyed information from the higher side to the earth plane. Every major religion started with communication from what we'd call an angel. The angel Gabriel came to Muhammad, the great prophet and founder of Islam, as he meditated and directed him to preach of the one god Allah. The Old Testament contains numerous accounts of people who were touched by the angelic realms and directed in their actions. In writings of ancient Judaism such as the Apocrypha and the Talmud, angels are fundamental messengers from God.

Today as well, there are people who have been open to experiencing communication with angels and those who have not. Their openness or not is related to their soul evolution and their purpose for incarnating. If your purpose for incarnating is for healing, you need to be able to connect to the higher realms so you can perform that healing work.

So part of the question becomes: "What is your purpose for coming to the earth plane?" If your purpose is to be the antagonist to get someone else to grow spiritually, then chances are, you're not so much knowingly in touch with the higher side but are just following along with what you're supposed to do. If your purpose is to serve, and especially to serve those on both the earth plane and the higher side, then yes, you will be very much in touch with the angels.

Try to hear the vague directions whispered in your ears, and find the road it seems you must follow.
—Zora Neale Hurston (1901–1960), American author

The very first time I saw Spirit, I saw it as pure light. That's what Spirit is, and there are times when I have seen Spirit energy appear vividly. As human beings, we are not accustomed to viewing energy in this way. More common to us are depictions and perceptions of angels appearing with beams of light radiating from behind them. Light is the presentation of pure energy; in natural form, the presence of angels is vibrational and energetic. Putting this presentation into human perspective gives rise to our perceptions of angels as winged beings with halos— we perceive the energy in light form that emanates from the angels in these ways. It's how our linear, logical minds want to categorize and define what we experience. These perceptions then become our expectations for how angels appear.

When I draw a spirit drawing for someone, it is a representation the person can recognize. The same is true with angels. Seeing them just as light and energy wouldn't make sense to us. We humans have to see something we can describe, classify, and explain. It's the nature of our existence as linear human beings. In a way, we can look at it as anthropomorphism—assigning human characteristics to nonhuman objects and experiences.

As humans defined by independent physical bodies, we find it difficult to comprehend the oneness of divine energy. We have difficulty accepting existence without the concept of linear time. However, there is no time in the spirit world. Time is for us because we keep trying to separate and classify. It's a human trait, not a spiritual trait. In the same way, we look to define nonphysical beings and experiences through physical traits. How spirit energy appears to us has to tap into us, to connect with what is in our memory banks.

Light Works: Angel Images

On a piece of heavier stock paper, draw a circle about the size of a dinner plate. Drizzle tempera paint inside the circle and then fold the paper in half. Now unfold it and let it dry.

After the paint is dry, take a moment to look at it and notice what images you see. Are there images telling you specifics about yourself? Are they telling you about the angels around you or about a specific angel?

How Angels Come to You and Make Their Presence Known

How do your angels connect to your life in tangible ways, to the energies that pull you and influence you? Angels appear in various, often subtle ways to different people. We have to learn to be aware of the presence of angels. Your angels have unique ways of communicating with you that connect to your base of experience and activate your memories. Your angels have to tap into what's in you so you can make sense of the messages they are bringing to you.

Even so, learning to communicate with your angels is a bit like learning a new language. It's not just that the angels need to find in us the connections we recognize. We need to tune in as well to be aware of these connections and to distinguish them as angelic communication.

The Perceptions of Your Physical Senses

Angel messages often activate our physical senses. They touch us through the activation of what is familiar to us. You might recognize a specific smell or other sensory experience you can't identify as someone specific, but you still know it's special. Maybe, as in the movie *Michael,* you smell chocolate-chip cookies. Some people see images, flashes of light and color, or shadows and shapes. Some people hear voices. Some people notice certain tastes. It is possible to have any or all your physical senses activated, just as they might be when experiencing the physical world. Angels might use whatever is a common way for you to experience your physical world to reach you. Over time, you learn that these are the signs that tell you your angels are present. This tangibility is for your benefit, to help you realize an angel's presence.

In the Light: Ask for Archangel Gabriel's Help to Express Your Truth

In Judaic, Islamic, and Christian writings, the archangel Gabriel appears as the messenger and bearer of divine truth. To the Mohammedans, Gabriel is the Spirit of Truth. The Kabbalists identify him as the man in linen, and rabbinic literature calls Gabriel the Prince of Justice. Christianity presents Gabriel as the angel who informs the Virgin Mary she is to be the mother of the Christ child Jesus. In John Milton's 12-book epic poem *Paradise Lost,* which depicts humankind's fall from grace, Gabriel sends the angelic guards to watch over Paradise.

Conveying messages of truth can be difficult. So many times we lock our truth inside. How many times have you wanted to say something to someone and were afraid that person just wouldn't hear you? How many times have you had questions and just couldn't find an answer? When you can realize your truth and speak it, a healing happens. Sometimes you can't deliver the message of this truth to the person you are hoping can hear it. Who will deliver the message to you or for you? Turn this over to the archangel Gabriel, who will enlist the aid of other angels to see that the message reaches its destination.

Write a truth, happy or difficult, you have been holding inside:

_____

_____

_____

Go into your sacred space or a place where you will not be disturbed and begin to meditate on this truth. Ask your angels and guides to be with you. Trust that they will be. Ask whatever questions seem unanswered for you, and ask for the answers to come. Write the questions here:

_____

_____

_____

Now release your unanswered questions or your unspoken truths to the Universe. Ask your angels to carry the truth to the Divine for the highest and the best. See it as done. Describe how this affects your life:

_____

_____

_____

The Perceptions of Your Intuitive Senses

We receive angel messages through our intuitive senses, through our perceptions. You might feel inspired or uplifted, such as when you're feeling a little sad and suddenly you feel like a warm blanket has been wrapped around you. Or you look up from your work to see a beautiful flower or a stunning sunset out your window. It's not the view itself that uplifts you but rather the moving of your mind into another state of perception. What you see is really the reflection of a divine presence. This experience can change your life for the moment or it can be overwhelming, because we as human beings sometimes get stuck in our own misery. Feeling the shift happen can bring tears to your eyes. These are spiritual gifts that come unexpectedly. I always say a great big thank you!

In the Light: Take Note of Daily Inspirations

Look up and out. How many times during a single day do you stop and allow yourself to be pulled to a beautiful, inspiring image? Over the course of one day, stop and record all the times this happens. Each time, thank your guides and angels. Then ask that these experiences be increased maybe one or two times a day. The angels will bring you back to this beautiful place we live called life. Allow it to happen.

Pictures and Metaphors

People often expect angels to speak to them in ordinary dialogue. Although angels can speak to us with unmistakable clarity, angel communication does not often take place in this way. More common are experiences and perceptions of images and messages we receive as bits of information such as thoughts or memories. We then have to put those bits together in ways that make sense for what is happening in our lives, like putting together a jigsaw puzzle. The more you work with your angels, the more quickly these pieces fall into place and the more quickly you develop a sense for the language of your angels.

In the Light: Making a Dream Pillow

One of the ways we can open our intuitive centers is by using colors and aromas. These elements can enhance our experiences and help us relax so we are much more open to receive. We know the dream state is a time when we put all the daily issues away. This is why the higher beings, spirit loved ones, and angels can connect with us with greater ease during these times. A dream pillow can blend colors and aromas to encourage angel communication during this receptive period. Because the higher chakras (your body's energy centers) facilitate spirit communication, we want to work with them in particular. Incorporate the following colors and herbs in your dream pillow to activate your higher chakras:

Chakra	Energy	Color	Herb
Heart	Emotions	Green or pink	Rose, jasmine
Throat	Truth and expression	Soft blue	Chamomile, sage, lemongrass
Brow	Inner vision ("third eye")	Deep blue/ violet	Rosemary, lavender, peppermint
Crown	Divine spirit	Violet	Frankincense (boswellia), myrrh, lavender

Your dream pillow need not be large; make it whatever size you like. You'll need a small piece of fabric (print or solid containing the colors of the chakras you want to stimulate), needle, thread, and the appropriate herbs. If you're not one for sewing, buy a small pouch you can fill with herbs and stitch or tie closed.

To make your dream pillow:

1. Cut a rectangle of fabric the size you desire.
2. Fold the fabric in half, right sides in, and sew it together on three sides.
3. Turn your fabric right side out, and press it with an iron.
4. Fill it with the appropriate herbs (individually or in combination).
5. Stitch closed the open side.

Place the dream pillow near your head when you are going to sleep. Don't be concerned about remembering your dreams. When you awake in the morning, you should feel a greater sense of peace with whatever issue you took to your angel. You also can use your dream pillow when you meditate to stimulate your chakras and encourage clear and open perception.

Exercising Your Intuitive Senses

Your intuitive perceptions—clairvoyance, clairaudience, and clairsentience—become more accurate the more you use them. As with your physical senses, your intuitive senses present you information about the messages that reach them. Your three intuitive senses correlate somewhat, although not precisely, to your physical senses. Some people receive messages through all their intuitive senses, but most people have one primary intuitive sense. Lower forms of energy activate your physical senses—light waves trigger nerve cells in your retinas, and sound waves trigger nerve cells in your inner ear. Higher forms of energy activate your intuitive senses. With practice, you can develop your abilities in all three intuitive senses—it's all about energy.

Clairvoyance is your inner vision, what we sometimes refer to as your "third eye." It allows you to perceive visual images that your brain interprets much the same way it might perceive the images that come to you through your physical eyes. Although there is an awareness that the image is not tangible, it has the appearance of being so.

Clairaudience is your inner hearing. People who hear the voices of their angels perceive them through clairaudience. As with clairvoyance, there is the awareness that the voices are not "real." Clairaudient messages often come in "sound bite" fashion; you hear segments that are somewhat like audible thoughts rather than individual words.

Clairsentience is the intuitive sense of knowing. People sometimes describe clairsentient experiences with "I feel" or "I just know." Some people perceive clairsentient experiences as ambiguous and indistinct yet undeniable. Other people perceive them as amalgamations of the whole, a blend of clairvoyance and clairaudience, that are almost tangible.

There is inside each of us a sixth sense: a soul sense which sees, hears, and feels all at the same time.
—Helen Keller (1880–1968), American writer

Each of us has a different way of experiencing intuitive messages. Those of us who are highly visual tend to get visual messages. People who tell stories to explain things receive messages in the form of stories. Those who are good at seeing the big picture or the whole story tend to receive clairsentient messages.

Angels Who Work Through You

Robert has been fighting cancer for more than 20 years and now has stage-four lung and liver cancer. Yet he's alive and well and passionate about life. If I hadn't known he was in chemotherapy, I would never have guessed he was so ill because he had a beautiful head of hair—unusual for someone in chemotherapy. In the cancer unit, he has become known as "Hurricane Robert" because he blows into the room with so much energy that he energizes everyone in there. "You have to fight this! You have to go on!" he exhorts as he goes from one person to another. His doctors can't believe he is so vibrant and full of life. He should have been on the higher side a long time ago, but with each round of treatment he becomes restored. Angels are touching Robert, and he is himself an angel touching the lives of so many others.

When Robert came to see me he said, "I am not going to die. I have too many reasons to live." He goes from chemotherapy to watch his daughter's horseback riding lesson or his son's baseball game. "I am going to stay alive for these children, and I want other people to know they, too, have many reasons to live," he says.

One of the stories he told me was of a woman in her late 80s whose family was all around her. She was crying because she couldn't get around on her own anymore. Robert went to her and told her, "Look at all the people around you, all the love you have surrounding you!" When Robert went back the next time, he found the woman up and walking around.

When Robert went to the doctor near the end of his current course of chemotherapy, the doctor was amazed to report that Robert had just two small spots on his lungs, which the remaining chemotherapy treatments would knock out. "How is this possible? How did you do this?" Robert's doctors marveled. And Robert marvels, too, because he knows it is the work of his angels, supporting him and keeping him alive to follow his lifepath.

Looking for the Lessons

It's easy to find comfort in Robert's story and stories like his, in the positive experiences people have with angelic influences in their lives. We can look at someone like Mother Teresa and see the tremendous good she brought to the earth plane, the many lives the divine touched through her work. Yet how comfortable do we feel when we consider that Mother Teresa and Adolf Hitler are of the same energy? Most of us want to reject such a premise without further consideration. The normal human response is to separate them immediately.

Yet these two beings are of the same energy, as we all are part of the divine. We learn and experience the divine from them both. Recognizing and accepting this concept is not easy when we look at Hitler and others like him. What do we learn from such individuals during their appearances as human beings? It is difficult for us to comprehend that they even bring us lessons, but they do. To discover the lesson is a process of exploring, not of pointing fingers and drawing conclusions. Angels and other higher beings come in and work with us to help us understand this and to learn our lessons.

There is a Secret One inside us; the planets in all the galaxies pass through His hands like beads.

—Kabir (1440–1518), Indian mystic and poet

In the Light: Embarking on New Adventures

As you travel your lifepath, you encounter new adventures and new challenges. How can you accommodate them without becoming overwhelmed with fear or apprehension? Ask your guides and angels to be with you. Ask for help. This is all part of the cycle of life. It's a new lesson, and you do not need to travel alone.

1. Visualize yourself walking into your new school, job, relationship, or other experience or situation.
2. Ask your angel, spirit guide, or loved one to be with you.
3. Visualize that the two of you are holding hands, smiling, walking together as you enjoy the experience.
4. Visualize the desired outcome.
5. Ask your angels, spirit guides, or loved ones: "What is necessary for me to achieve this?"
6. Listen to the answer with your spirit, not your brain.
7. See it as done.

Fear Not the Angelic Encounter

Much of our Western-culture association with angels has to do with the context of death and passing from the earth plane to the higher side. Many people report encounters with angels during near-death experiences. From belief systems to movies such as *City of Angels,* there is an association between angels and death. As much as anything, this probably reflects our worries and fears about dying and the mystery of what awaits us beyond physical death. Angels seem to have clear roles in helping us with the earth plane transitions of both birth and death. Spiritualists believe that when a baby is born the people on the earth plane celebrate while those on the higher side cry because they've lost one of their own. But when a person dies, people on the earth plane cry while those on the higher side celebrate as they welcome the one back.

When we connect to the love that comes from the higher side, when we feel it, we know we are safe. I have never experienced fear from anything coming from the higher side. It has always been presented in love, in goodness, in a way that is nurturing. Angels are presentations of this loving energy, helping us look past existence on the earth plane to the oneness of energy that connects us all.

In Chapter 1, we created the angel card *Oneness* to remind us of this. And we all need to be reminded at times. In Chapter 2, I told the story of sitting at the end of the bed with my dear friend Eric, knowing he had just a few days to remain on the earth plane. I needed to know he would be okay even though I know there is an afterlife. A glorious angel appeared. Loving and beautiful, she embraced him, and I watched as this took place. It moved me to tears because it was not what I expected to see from an angel of death. But Spirit knew I needed assurance that Eric was being taken care of and so presented me with this image that was totally warm, soft, and loving. And then I knew, without question, that Eric would be cared for.

Light Works: Chapter 4 Angel Card

This chapter's angel card word is *Essence*. We are all part of the divine. That is the thread that ties us together; it is our essence, the core of our being. Think, go into a meditation, and see the image of *your* true essence. Find the Divine within your essence. Using colors, shapes, and other elements of design that appeal to you, create that image on your *Essence* angel card.

Highest and Best: Inspired Writing

All information is accessible to the higher mind. One way you can open yourself to this information is through inspired writing in which you allow your angels, spirit guides, or loved ones to send you messages through writing. You are not the author of this writing; this is angelic communication—*your* angels. For this exercise, you need some paper or your journal.

1. Go to your sacred place or to another place that is quiet where you will not be interrupted. You need room or a surface where you can comfortably write as well as a pen and paper. You might want to tape-record this meditation first and follow its guidance as you go to meet your inner angel.

2. Begin by taking three deep breaths, in through your nose and out through your mouth. Take a deep breath in through your nose to clear your body, then release it. Take a second breath to open your mind and a third breath to free your spirit.

3. Think now of the questions you want answered or what situations are creating challenges in your life. Write them at the top of your paper.

4. Ask your angels, spirit guides, or loved ones to send you the answers or the information you are seeking. When you feel you are ready, allow yourself to begin writing.

5. Write freely whatever comes to you. Hold nothing back, and don't worry if what you're writing seems to make no sense. Just let the writing come out. Keep writing until you feel you are finished.

6. When the inspired writing is done, pick up the paper and read out loud the answers you received. When you read, follow the flow of the writing without attempting to make corrections or edit the words. Listen to the words, and try to envision the images of the messages they bring to you. Let your mind make whatever connections it wants to make.

7. Now write some perceptions about the inspired writing messages you received. Can you relate them to the events or questions you asked about? If not, don't worry. You have still received the answers; it just might take you some time to understand what they are. If the messages seem truly disconnected from what you were asking, either repeat the exercise or perhaps consider that you really were asking something else.

Your angels and spirit guides appear to you in ways that you will understand and accept. They present themselves in images—visual as well as expressive—that are familiar and comforting. When you can use all your senses—physical and intuitive—you open yourself to receiving the Divine guidance your angels bring you. What you see, hear, feel, and otherwise sense as the presence of angels is unique to you and your experiences and perceptions of the Divine.

Chapter 5

Expressions of Divine Energy

In 1985, I was teaching art to troubled kids. One of my students was a young man named Derrick. On his first day, Derrick walked into my classroom with his head down. He was very sad. I wanted to get through to him, but he wouldn't talk and he wouldn't work. He just sat through class with his head down on his desk. After about half an hour of this I said to him, "Hey, if I draw your picture, will you do some work for me?" Derrick picked up his head and studied me for a moment. "Sure, you can draw me," he said.

So I drew his picture, a charcoal drawing, and I handed it to him. This sad young man scrutinized the picture for a few minutes, then a big grin came to his face. "Okay, I'll work for you," he said. And he did. Every time he came to class he worked. He wasn't always the easiest student; art was not his forte. But he tried, and he did the work.

At first I thought it was I who was helping Derrick, but as it turned out, the reverse was just as true. At the time, I was between series as an artist. I had just finished a series of expressionist portraits and had no idea what to do next. When I went into meditation and asked my guides what I should do, they told me to work with the kids. So I started photographing and drawing my students, and I knew immediately this was to be my next series.

Rita's charcoal drawing Well, My Young Man.

And as it had been for him, Derrick's drawing became a spark for me. It inspired the first in what was to become an eight-year series of drawings and paintings for me—my *City Folks* series, one of my most successful works as an artist.

And what about Derrick? He had a long road. He was in and out of trouble during his teenage years. He would often call me, and I would ask him how he was doing. He would say, "Rita, I'm staying out of trouble." It was as if staying out of trouble was his full-time job. Very recently he entered a state program to study culinary arts, and he now has a job working as a chef. He calls me every now and then, and I am grateful to him for being an angel in my life ... and in my art.

Divine Inspiration

As much as angels are the subjects of works of art, they also inspire the work. I think of it somewhat like the chicken and the egg: What came first, the art or the inspiration? You must have one to have the other.

Divine inspiration is our muse; it comes and we create. So when we talk about angels in art, we're not talking about angels just as the familiar Renaissance-style winged beings. We're talking about angels coming to us and working through us in the creativity of our everyday lives. We are all creative in our own ways, no matter what we do for a living or where we find joy in our lives. We become inspired and then we do the work to make manifest the creation of that inspiration.

Rita's drawing Which Way Do I Go?

English poet Robert Browning (1812–1889) found Divine inspiration through the angel that appeared in the work of another artist. Browning, who lived in Italy for most of his adult life, was in the Italian town of Fano when he saw the painting *The Guardian Angel* by Baroque painter Giovanni Francesco Barbieri Guerchin (1591–1666), known as Guercino (you can view Guercino's beautiful painting online at www.browninglibrary. org/jonesartifacts.htm and more of Guercino's work, including numerous angel paintings, at www.artcyclopedia.com).

The painting captivated Browning, who returned several times to see it and then wrote a poem about it, "The Guardian Angel: A Picture at Fano." In his poem, Browning wishes for the painting's guardian angel to leave its post on the canvas and come into his life to help him see the world with clarity and depth so he might capture its views in his own creative work as Guercino did in his:

> I think how I should view the earth and skies
> And sea, when once again my brow was bared
> After thy healing, with such different eyes.
> O world, as God has made it! All is beauty:
> And knowing this, is love, and love is duty.
> What further may be sought for or declared?

In my own work, I let the angels take my hand and guide me. Every morning before I begin my day, I ask my most high guides and the master artists to be with me throughout the day when I'm doing my work. I allow the beautiful spiritual energy to come through. One step informs the next ... this is inspired work. We all can do this, no matter what the endeavor. It's all connected, and through it, we are all connected. Divine inspiration is within us all. Where is yours leading you? Are you following its direction?

Light Works: Chapter 5 Angel Card

This chapter's angel card word is *Manifest*. What do we want and need in our lives to serve our highest and best? Sometimes we so strongly doubt that the higher forces will work with us that we won't even ask. But they will help us when we ask. Go into your mind and visualize the colors, shapes, and movement of pure creativity. Imagine what that feels like, and ask your guides and angels to help you make this manifest in your life. Now, create your angel card for *Manifest*.

Creative Visions: Angels in Art

Works of art depicting angels are numerous and date from the ancient cultures of Mesopotamia, Greece, the Roman Empire, and Egypt. The belief systems and mythologies of these cultures featured winged deities whom scholars believe became the basis for religious representations of angels—messengers of the divine—across cultures. From about 2900 B.C.E., we have Sumerian sculptures of winged creatures archaeologists believe adorned the walls of ancient temples. These sculptures are all that remain of the spiritual practices of this culture. Fleet-footed Mercury, messenger of the gods, appears throughout Roman mythology as one who leads humans astray and then himself escapes the consequences (and the wrath of the Heavens) with the aid of his winged heels and his winged thoughts.

Carvings of winged creatures dating to around 400 B.C.E. have been found along the Bering Straits, reflecting the integration of nature and Spirit that characterized the belief systems of the indigenous tribes that inhabited the upper reaches of the North American and Asian continents. The intricate detail of these carvings, typically of walrus ivory, presents pictorial stories of great hunts and messages that appear to be thanks given to the Divine for releasing the spirits of hunted seals and other animals. Ceremonial masks representing Divine images are common in many cultures of early civilizations, extending from the North Atlantic to the South Pacific Oceans.

Angels appear in the illuminated manuscripts of medieval times (sixth to early fourteenth centuries). The mystic cards of the Tarot, believed to have originated in the eighth or ninth century, incorporate angels. Archangel Gabriel appears on the Judgement card and Archangel Michael on the Temperance card, and angel representations also appear on various Minor Arcana cards. By the Renaissance (late fourteenth to mid-sixteenth centuries), sacred and angelic themes came to dominate art (as well as music, literature, and philosophy) in the Western world. Following the darkness and despair of the Middle Ages, during which life was a struggle against famine, poor living conditions, and disease throughout the Western world, the Renaissance heralded an emergence into the light. There was much to be thankful for, and artists across the spectrum offered gratitude in abundance through their creative endeavors.

Paintings and sculptures that have survived from this productive creativity are now on display in museums, cathedrals, small churches, and private collections throughout the world. Via one of the great wonders of modern technology—the Internet—we can see these grand masterpieces without leaving home. If you can see the original artwork, do it. There is no substitute for feeling the energy of the painting or seeing the drama of the work as the artist created it.

When you cannot see the real thing, let the Internet take you to the virtual art. Here are some of my favorite Italian Renaissance and Baroque works, with websites where you can "travel" to enjoy them for yourself. (Sometimes websites change; if the website you want to display is no longer valid, type the name of the work of art or of the artist into your web browser to find another website.)

The Ecstasy of S. Teresa di Avila is a collection of inspired sculptures done by Giovanni Lorenzo Bernini (1598–1680) that fills the

Cornaro Chapel in Rome's Church of S. Maria della Vittoria. The display features a carved stage with the statues of an angel visiting St. Teresa. Marble sculpture likenesses of church officials look on from balconies above the stage as the officials themselves did in Bernini's time. Each statue is nearly 12 feet tall and depicts Teresa's account of her encounter with the angel and the resulting ecstasy of spirit that consumed her. Visitors to the Cornaro Chapel find the display awe-inspiring. You can view selected images of Bernini's extraordinary work at www.boglewood.com/cornaro/xteresa.html.

The Annunciation, the event in which the archangel Gabriel announces to the Virgin Mary that she is to be the mother of the child Jesus, is a popular subject of Renaissance angel paintings. Among the most popular of such paintings is the one by the Dominican friar Fra Angelico, born Guido di Pietro (1395–1455). Titled simply *The Annunciation* (or even *Annunciation*), Fra Angelico's rendition of this sacred event shows a glorious Gabriel talking to a youthful and somewhat overwhelmed Mary. To see this painting online, go to www.italian-art.org/masters/fra_angelico/art.html and select one of the two *Annunciation* images to view the enlargement. Be sure to look at both paintings, which Fra Angelico did 18 years apart. Many Renaissance as well as modern artists painted the Annunciation; use your web browser to search for their works or visit a website such as www.artcyclopedia.com. To look at the many artistic interpretations of this event is interesting and fun. How many variations can you find?

Caravaggio's *The Inspiration of St. Matthew* is one of the most famous paintings of the Renaissance, more for its technique than its subject matter although I find both intriguing. Matthew sits, quill in hand, awestruck as the archangel Gabriel dictates to him the words of God. Caravaggio (full name Michelangelo Merisi da Caravaggio, 1573–1610) pioneered the style of dramatic realism of this painting, which was commissioned for the Contarelli Chapel in the Church of San Luigi dei Francesi in Rome, where it remains on display today. You can see this dramatic painting online at www.ibiblio.org/wm/paint/auth/caravaggio/. Other famous Caravaggio paintings featuring angels are *The Death of the Virgin* and *Amor Victorious*. When you look at collections in art books and on the web, see what other works by Caravaggio you find that display this painter's divine inspiration.

Other classic angel paintings include Sandro Botticelli's *Magnificat Madonna,* numerous works by the prolific Michelangelo (among the most notable paintings being *The Last Judgment, Creation of Adam,* and *Temptation and Expulsion*), Gustave Doré's *Jacob Wrestling the Angel,* and (one of my personal favorites) *Musical Angels* by Flemish painter Hans Memling (sometimes spelled Memlinc). www.artcyclopedia.com features images and information about these and numerous other works of art. The site also has links to museums, churches and chapels, and other online sources for works of angel art from the early fourteenth century to modern times. Do you see other paintings, sculptures, and works of art that capture your interest?

Angels remain popular subjects for artists in our modern times. Many artists portray angelic representations in their work, from traditional images to stylized renditions in a variety of media, even electronic. And angels adorn everything from greeting cards to T-shirts.

Some 70 years after his death, American painter Abbott Handerson Thayer (1849–1921) got his angel on the cover of the December 27, 1993, issue of *Time* magazine. The painting, done in 1887 and simply titled *Angel,* is said to be a portrait of Thayer's eldest daughter, Mary. Thayer portrayed real people, often his daughters, as winged guardian angels. Another popular Thayer angel painting is 1903's *The Stevenson Memorial,* a tribute to writer Robert Louis Stevenson. The Smithsonian American Art Museum in Washington, D.C., displays these and other Thayer paintings on its website at www.nmaa.si.edu/treasures/bios/ 04766.html.

See the surrealistic works of Salvador Dali, such as *The Vision of the Angel* sculpture and Dali's numerous paintings of angels (including Dali's variation of the Annunciation), at www.daligallery.com. How do you react to some of these highly stylized renditions?

Travel into the whimsical dreamscapes of New York artist Sheila Wolk at www.heavenandearthdesigns.com. And explore the computer-enhanced, award-winning images of Northwest illustrator Corey Wolfe at www.coreywolfe.com. There are hundreds, if not thousands, of contemporary angel images; look for others that are in styles similar to that of Wolk or Wolfe, or follow the links on these websites to view the works of other artists.

There is no shortage of angels in art, and you don't have to travel farther than your computer to view and enjoy them. Do certain styles and artists appeal to you? Why? Can you feel or otherwise detect the artist's inspiration as you view the art? What messages do your favorite works of art seem to be conveying? Do you feel the message is personal to you?

Discovery consists of seeing what everybody has seen and thinking what nobody has thought.

—Albert Szent-Gyorgyi (1893–1986), Hungarian-born physician awarded the 1937 Nobel Prize in Physiology or Medicine

In the Light: Art Explorations

From your art explorations, choose one work of angel art that particularly captivates your interest and research it. Who is the artist? Why did he or she create this work? Why use this medium? What influences—artistic, cultural, social, spiritual, religious—might have shaped the artist's presentation? What have others (such as critics and curators) said about this work? What appeals to you about the piece? What story does the work tell you? Are your personal interpretations similar to those of others and to the artist's intent (if this is known)? What other works featuring angels has the same artist done? Do those works convey the same intent and mood? Are they done in similar style? Do they interest you as well? You might want to keep an art journal to record your perceptions and responses to the art and artists you explore.

Don't worry, these questions have no right or wrong answers. When I teach art, I like to encourage my students to look beyond the drawing or painting to gain deeper understanding about the choices the artist makes when creating the work. Sometimes an artist creates several renditions of the same image, as Fra Angelico did with *The Annunciation,* for example, and Salvador Dali with a number of his drawings and paintings. Art is an exploration for the artist, too. And as the artist grows and develops, so does his or her creative vision. An early work might be strikingly different from a later work that features the same subject, reflecting the artist's creative as well as spiritual evolution. Your perceptions also might change over time or as your understanding and acceptance deepen.

Angels of Celebration

Angels or angel-like representations became associated with spiritual and religious traditions, festive celebrations, and special occasions in ancient times. Sumerians and Babylonians, societies of 2500 to 1500 B.C., decorated their temples with carvings and statues of winged beings representing their gods and the seven heavens in which the gods resided. Some appear with discs behind their heads, believed to indicate the sun (the supreme ruler and giver of life in ancient mythologies), giving the being its celestial essence. Later we see this imagery adapted as the traditional halo that encircles the heads of angels and other sacred or holy figures, coming to represent the heavenly or divine.

Some celebrations have moved through different traditions over the centuries. Cupid, the winged messenger of love we associate today with Valentine's Day, originated in Greek mythology as the god Eros, the lusty deity of desire. In his migration to Roman mythology, which tended to present a softer and what we might today call more socially acceptable view of the universe, Eros became Cupid, the son of Venus, the goddess of love. As her son, Cupid became the emissary of love. This mythology became mixed in medieval times with pagan celebrations of the onset of spring and its corresponding mating season as well as with religious traditions honoring several martyrs each known as Saint Valentine. Renaissance representations of Cupid typically featured an angelic boy with a bow and arrow, the image of Cupid that persists today.

Angels also feature prominently in the Christian celebration of Christmas. The tradition of the angel on top of the Christmas tree is a reminder of the story of the Annunciation, the subject of so many works of art in which an angel came to tell Mary she was to bear the child Jesus, and of the message of the birth itself, in which an angel appears to announce the birth of Jesus to a group of shepherds.

Light Works: Create an Angel Art Scrapbook

Greeting cards for all occasions feature angels. The next time you are in a store that sells greeting cards, peruse the different categories. Look at what images appear on the various kinds of cards. If you've been going to the websites to look at the works of the masters (or have art books with their images), what works do you recognize on greeting cards? How do greeting card manufacturers integrate the angel images with the text of the card?

Start a scrapbook of angel art from greeting cards—it's an easy and inexpensive way to collect images from the classic masters to the contemporary. Go to your favorite crafts store or variety store and buy a scrapbook with a plain cover. Photo albums with slip-in pockets or "magnetic" (electrostatic) pages also work well, or you can use heavy sheets of paper in an ordinary three-ring notebook. Put the card in the book and write a few comments about the artist, the intended purpose of the card (birthday, religious events and holidays, sympathy, encouragement), and your reactions to its artwork.

Create a decoupage cover for your scrapbook that features cut-out images from magazines, wrapping paper, newspapers, and other found images. Glue the images to your scrapbook cover or to a piece of cardboard with rubber cement or paper cement (these cements hold better than school glue). When you're finished, seal your collage with clear acrylic gloss gel medium (buy this at any art or craft supply store) applied with a clean brush. (It goes on dull but dries clear.)

Angels in Writing

In Chapter 3, we invited the angels to communicate with you directly. The angelic being Elucia responded and spoke through me while I was in a state of trance, taking use of my voice. As I shared with you in Chapter 3, the experience of "hosting" the Divine in my body, of being so infused with the energy of the Divine, was what I can only describe as awesome—nearly overwhelming. I can't even imagine what an experience it must have been for the prophet Muhammad when Archangel Gabriel, the Divine messenger, appeared to Muhammad to reveal the 114 *surahs,* or chapters, of the Koran, the Divine document that became the foundation of Islam. The Koran, a modern term for the Arabic word *Qur'an,* means "the recitation."

According to Islamic tradition, Gabriel entered Muhammad's heart while the prophet was in a trancelike state. Gabriel filled all Muhammad's senses until all that Muhammad could experience was Gabriel's presence. In such a state, Muhammad received the chapters of the Koran, which, although Muhammad lived in a time when few people could read or write (historians dispute whether Muhammad was among them), he recorded as Gabriel instructed. Gabriel's Divine dictation took place over the span of 20 years. Muhammad wrote his original recitations on fragments of leather and palm leaves, the materials available to him. Imagery of and references to angels, which are fundamental in the Muslim faith, fill the Koran. After Muhammad's death the writings were gathered into book form, although for centuries it remained the practice to recite the surahs. Manuscripts of the Koran, handwritten in Arabic, exist that date to the seventeenth century.

The visual arts were the predominant presentation of angels for many centuries until literacy became commonplace. The illuminated manuscripts of the medieval period were the first presentations to combine images with words. Elaborate etchings, originally made of gold and silver and later incorporating pigments used in painting, sometimes overwhelmed the pages of the handwritten books of the time (the word *manuscript* means "written by hand").

In 1307, Italian poet Dante Alighieri (1265–1321) started his three-part masterpiece *Divina Commedia* (*The Divine Comedy*) and completed it shortly before his death 14 years later. The epic poem follows its narrator's travels through Hell (Part 1, *Inferno*), Purgatory (Part 2, *Purgatorio*), and Heaven (Part 3, *Paradiso*). The epic's rich imagery features spirit guides (including Virgil, the great Greek poet) and numerous angels who escort the narrator on his spiritual journey. At the journey's end, the narrator becomes one with the light and the joy of the divine and, although still human, stands as one with the divine. *The Divine Comedy* has inspired the works of numerous artists in visual media—among them Sandro Botticelli, Gustave Doré, and Salvador Dali.

The epic poem *Paradise Lost* by English poet John Milton (1608–1674) is another magnificent exploration of the realms of Heaven and the guidance of angels. Written in 12 books, *Paradise Lost* tells the story of the conquest of the Garden of Eden by the fallen angels under Satan's leadership. The archangels Gabriel and Raphael try to save Paradise, but ultimately Satan defeats them through deceit. The story is fairly biblical; the imagery, like Dante's, is vivid.

English poet William Blake (1757–1827), also a talented painter and illustrator, incorporated angels and mystic imagery in nearly all of his work. As an apprentice engraver early in his career, Blake illustrated an edition of Dante's *The Divine Comedy;* later in his career he illustrated his own poems. *The Book of Thel* and *The Marriage of Heaven and Hell* are among Blake's most exploratory works and reflect his fascination with the mystic. Blake drew from the religious traditions of his time although he presented unique, and sometimes controversial, interpretations of them.

Robert Louis Stevenson, Edgar Allan Poe, H. G. Wells, Leo Tolstoy, and Flannery O'Connor all wrote stories about angels. In his short story "A Very Old Man with Enormous Wings," Gabriel García Márquez (who won the 1982 Nobel Prize in Literature) tells the tale of an angel come to Earth to take the soul of a sick child who instead crashes to the ground. Apparently the victim of his own old age and the terrible weather conditions, he is taken captive by the villager into whose yard he lands. The villager exploits the angel, charging visitors to see him and eventually acquiring enough money to build a large mansion with bars on the windows to keep the angels from falling in, as the one already living with them had become a nuisance. As the child recovers and grows up, interest in the angel gradually wanes. One day he stands in the courtyard and spreads his wings, and the wind carries him up and away—and no one notices he is gone or remembers that he was even there.

And of course, there are numerous stories and poems for children that feature angels—some lighthearted and delightful, others that tackle difficult subjects such as dying.

Light Works: Make a Memory Mandala

A mandala is a circle that contains a patterned design, usually geometric and symmetrical, which can be used to help you focus and meditate. A mandala can be highly abstract or include images that are tangible representations. A memory mandala is a unique design that you create to honor your angels. It can be as simple or as complex as you choose to make it. To get started you'll need:

- A piece of heavy paper or light cardboard from which you can cut a circle that is 6 to 12 inches in diameter
- Scissors
- Colored markers, pencils, crayons, or paints
- Construction paper, coloraide paper, or craft tissue
- Glue or paper cement

Draw a circle on the paper and cut it out. Draw, color, or paint designs on your circle. Build your images from the center out or from the circumference (outer edge) in. Try to maintain a sense of balance in the way you place the designs to keep the overall look of your mandala symmetrical.

Your images can be literal or symbolic. Let your intuition and your creativity take control, and glue or tape the images onto your mandala. Place them where they feel right to you. You can cut apart images to make your mandala more abstract or group them to make your mandala more tangible.

When you're finished, go to your sacred place or a quiet location where you can sit for a few minutes without being disturbed. Hold your mandala in your hands. What do you see when you look at it? What do you feel? If you like, meditate with your mandala. Focus on the imagery and pattern of your mandala until that's all that fills your mind. Let your mind fully explore what the mandala brings to it. When you are ready to release your meditation, allow your focus to gradually expand until you are again aware of your surroundings and other thoughts.

*Your memory mandala can be as simple
or complex as you like.*

Choirs of Angels

I am a visual artist and a clairvoyant medium; primarily I see or envision
the spirits that present themselves, then draw their images. Sometimes I
detect fragrances and smells such as perfume or cigar smoke characteris-
tic of the spirit during its earthly existence. Occasionally I hear music
as well. Many times spirits will come in with a line of song that had a
definite, personal meaning for the person and the loved one who is communicating. Loved ones often connect with us through the memory of
music because songs bring us back to special times, places, and events.
They can be validation of the communication and the message it brings.

Music, it's been said, is the language of the soul. We use it to set the
mood in various situations in our lives. We use music at weddings, funerals, church services, and celebrations of all kinds. Music lets us express,
without words, our emotions and feelings and keys us in to the emotions
and feelings of others. I use music in my work as a spiritual medium, just
as I use candles (light) and aromatherapy (fragrances). These elements
raise the vibration to help us connect with the higher realms.

One morning in church, a man gave me a tape to play for the healing service. He told me, "This is the music people hear when they go to the higher side." I played the tape for the service, and it was beautiful. After the service, a woman came to talk to me. She had a look of astonishment on her face. "Where did you get that music?" she asked. I told her. "Seven years ago I had a near-death experience and I heard that music!" she said.

The horn or trumpet has long symbolized communication with the divine and spirit communication. In angel art, the trumpet represents communication from God; the archangel Gabriel, the divine messenger, often appears with one. The trumpet also was the instrument of message in early societies, heralding pronouncements from the king and calling citizens to gather.

The harp is another instrument commonly associated with angels. This is a difficult instrument to master because its strings resonate with each other, producing overlays of tone that can sound painfully cacophonous or beautifully harmonious. In ancient Greek mythology, the Muses (daughters of Zeus) often were represented playing the lyre, a stringed instrument somewhat between a harp and a guitar in sound. The sweetness of their music, according to myth, inspired poets and artists. In later centuries, more elaborate instruments such as the harp replaced the lyre among musicians and in artistic renditions of angels.

Singing is a key form of musical expression when it comes to the angels. Sacred writings often refer to choirs of angels, and people who have near-death experiences often report hearing sounds of music and singing that are too beautiful to describe. And of course, singing is the one form of musical expression that requires no instrument beyond the human voice. Everyone can join voices in song, even if those voices are less than angelic!

Much music, instrumental and lyric, through the centuries has attempted to express or address the spiritual and the sacred, from the compositions of Bach and Mozart to contemporary songs from Sarah McLachlan ("In the Arms of the Angels").

It is the function of creative men to perceive the relations between thoughts, or things, or forms of expression that may seem utterly different, and to be able to combine them into some new forms—the power to connect the seemingly unconnected.
—William Plomer (1903–1973), British poet and writer

Hollywood's Angels

And I'm not talking about Charlie's angels here! Angels have been popular in the movies since the early days of film, serving as vehicles to explore the many quandaries of human (and heavenly) existence as well as to celebrate the joy of living. Here are some of Hollywood's angel movies. Most are available on videotape or DVD for home viewing. If your local video store doesn't stock the ones you want to watch, see if your public library might have them (especially the older black-and-white movies). You also can rent videos through Internet-based services.

Here Comes Mr. Jordan (1941) and the subsequent remakes *Heaven Can Wait* (1978) and *Down to Earth* (2001) all give variations on the theme of a soul being taken to heaven before its time and the efforts to make it right. Rent all three and compare their presentations. Aside from differences related to the times the movies were produced, what in the story lines changed? Which version appeals to you?

A perennial holiday favorite, the classic *It's a Wonderful Life* (1946) stars James Stewart as bank officer George Bailey and Henry Travers as Clarence Oddbody, AS2 (Angel Second Class). When George despairingly wishes he'd never been born, Clarence shows him what life would have been like had that been the case. The black-and-white original has been colorized in the version shown on television and available on videotape.

An angel comes to earth to rectify a mistake in heaven's *Book of Life* that allows a gambling Montana rancher to live as though he has no soul in *Heaven Only Knows*. The angel must help the gambler change his ways and discover that he does indeed have a soul. The movie presents an odd blend of the angel theme and old-style western. When you watch this movie, how well do you think this blend works?

In *The Bishop's Wife* (1947; starring Cary Grant, David Niven, and Loretta Young) and its 1996 remake *The Preacher's Wife* (with Denzel Washington, Whitney Houston, and Courtney B. Vance), heaven sends an angel ostensibly to help the congregation but really to get the man of the cloth's marriage back on track.

The angels enjoy the competition of the all-American sport, baseball, in *Angels in the Outfield* (1951; featuring Paul Douglas, Janet Leigh with cameos by Ty Cobb, Joe DiMaggio, and Bing Crosby) and the 1994 remake (with Tony Danza, Danny Glover, and Christopher Lloyd). In both, a nasty manager changes his ways as angelic intervention improves the team even though a child is the only one who sees the angels in the outfield making the plays.

In 1985's *The Heavenly Kid,* a cocky teen dies when the car he's racing goes off a cliff. However, he cannot complete his journey to heaven until he serves as a guardian angel for the nerdish youth he used to pick on. In a similar vein is *Almost an Angel* (1990) with Paul Hogan as an ex-con who's hit by a car while saving another man from the same fate and ends up an "angel on probation."

Exploring the possibility that humans also help angels is 1987's *Date with an Angel,* in which an angel falls into the swimming pool at a bachelor party and the bachelor safeguards her while she returns to health. *Date with an Angel* is a remake of the 1942 musical *I Married an Angel.*

Angels listen to the thoughts of humans, step in to provide protection and comfort, and escort the souls of those who die in 1988's *Wings of Desire* and its 1998 remake *City of Angels* with Nicolas Cage and Meg Ryan. What is it like to be human, the angels wonder—to touch, to taste, to smell, to feel happiness and pain? They can choose to find out, but they must give up their symbolic wings—and literally, then must fall—to do so. It's common to think about people who desire to become angels and somewhat of a different perspective to think about angels who want to become human. How do you feel about this?

The angels revolt in 1995's *The Prophecy.* Christopher Walken portrays an angry Gabriel who becomes frustrated with the attention God gives to humans who are undeserving of it. He decides to take matters into his own hands and rallies a force of angels to destroy humankind. First, however, the angel army must do battle with heaven's good angels. Sequels *The Prophecy II* (1998) and *The Prophecy III* (2000) continue the story.

The archangel Michael enjoys a final visit on Earth in the 1996 movie *Michael,* with John Travolta in the starring role. He spends the last days with a team of reporters from a scandal-sheet newspaper who have heard that he is an angel and want to do a feature story about him. What the team doesn't know is that part of Michael's mission in his final incarnation is to help them regain their core qualities of goodness. Travolta's Michael is more earthy than most representations—he smokes, he eats sugared cereal by the boxful, and women find him (or that he smells like chocolate-chip cookies) irresistible. Some viewers find the earthy Michael a bit much to accept as an angel, however. What do you think of Travolta's Michael? Does it feel plausible in the context of the movie?

Loki and Bartleby, a pair of fallen angels, conspire to take advantage of an opportunity to return to heaven in 1999's dark comedy *Dogma,* with Matt Damon and Ben Affleck in the starring roles and singer Alanis Morissette as God. If the pair can pull off their planned act of vengeance against humankind, they prove God wrong and cause the end of all existence.

Incredible performances by Meryl Streep, Al Pacino, Emma Thompson, Mary-Louise Parker, and Justin Kirk bring from the stage to the small screen this intense epic in which an angel comes to Earth and tells a gay man dying of AIDS that he is a prophet in *Angels in America* (2003), a film that won four Golden Globe Awards.

It's fun to look at all these presentations of angels, particularly across the span of time they cover. What are your favorite three movies about angels, either those listed here or others? How are they different, and how are they similar in the ways they portray angels? Are these presentations consistent with what you perceive about angels? How do you feel about the presentations? Write a review that compares your three favorites.

Highest and Best: Presenting Your Angels

Who are the angels in your life? We hear so much talk about the Archangels, who they are, and what they stand for. Each has a unique purpose or role, and if we look at them as archetypes, we can find people in our lives—parent, sibling, teacher, clergy, therapist, colleague, or good friend—who represent each of them:

- **Archangel Michael** ranks the greatest of all the angels. He represents righteousness, mercy, and deliverance. Write a few sentences about a person in your life who always comes through for you when you are in need. Think of your larger life.

- **Archangel Gabriel** is known as the Spirit of Truth in Christian, Judaic, and Islamic traditions. He sits at the left hand of God, a position of trust and confidence, and conveys messages to and from God. Think of a person in your life whose counsel you can count on. Who sits at your left hand? Write a few sentences about the person in your life that you can truly talk to on an intimate level, the person who can listen to you and give you the truth about what you might be discussing.

- **Archangel Raphael** is known as the healer of the masses and of the earth as a whole. Think of a person, public or private, who you consider a great healer, one who has done service to humanity in a large or small way. Write how you feel about the person's work.
- **Archangel Uriel** presides over repentance. Where do you go for help in letting go of burdens you are carrying? Write a few sentences describing the process that you use to release the burdens of the past.

Chapter 6

Recognizing Angels at Work in Your Life

Who are those people in our lives who always seem to be there to carry us in times of need? They are our angels. Sometimes we know who they are, and sometimes we have unlikely angels. The unlikely angels might be people we never expect to do anything to change our lives. We don't always stop to think about who these people are. They don't have to be profound people; they don't have to be people who have great credentials. They are there when unexpectedly wonderful things happen, and they often seem to be the deliverers of important—and joyous—messages. These are the people who touch our lives in ways we always remember.

When I was a young child, I contracted rheumatic fever, which was a serious and debilitating disease at the time that attacked my joints. The inflammation and swelling in my knees and hips and back were so destructive, that a number of doctors who were specialists in this disease examined me and sadly pronounced that I would not walk again. However, one doctor would not give up on my condition and came to my house every morning to check on me. He moved my arms and legs, bending and extending my stiff and swollen joints. He gently joked with me to distract me and to keep me believing that I would get better. He was determined to make me well, to make sure I would one day feel ready to get up and walk again—and be able to do it. One morning I did just that, and he was the one jumping up and down, shouting, "It's a miracle!" Even as a child, I knew I had been touched with the Divine energy of this one man's dedication and effort. I can vividly recall the persistence in his eyes and the compassion in his touch. I can still see him at my front door the first time I walked to answer it. He was truly an angel in my life.

> But men must know that in this theater of man's life it is reserved only for God and angels to be lookers on.
> —Francis Bacon (1561–1626), English philosopher

Our relationships with the people who are angels in our lives have an emotional quality that creates powerful bonds between us. The presence of some is fleeting, but there are others who remain connected to us and help us not only make it through difficult challenges but also learn and grow in the process. We might think we are actually helping some of these people when in fact they are helping us. Can you look at your own life and see people who have touched it in simple ways to change it profoundly for the better?

Be Not Afraid: Overcoming Fear

Fear is a big factor in the lives of many people because we fear many things. When our fears generate a healthy respect for risk or danger, this is good fear. This respect helps us act with prudence and caution. All too often, however, our fears keep us from becoming who we are and all we can be. But what is fear, and what do we fear? You might answer, "Plenty!" and you wouldn't be wrong. But as Franklin D. Roosevelt (1882–1945), thirty-second president of the United States, famously asserted in his inaugural address, "The only thing we have to fear is fear itself!"

Much of what we fear is not people or events. Mostly we fear change, even when it clearly is for the better. Change presents us with unknowns, and the unknown can be scary. Even when the known is unpleasant and even harmful, at least we know what to expect—and there is comfort in that expectation. Yet life is about change. Remember from Chapter 3, that the higher being Elucia tells us it is the true essence of each of us that craves the lessons we are in this life to learn. When we lose track of this—as sometimes we human beings do—we find ourselves fearful. We worry about what others might be thinking and saying about us, yet one reason we are here is to overcome these feelings so we follow our lifepaths with confidence and faith rather than resist in fear. The only obstacle we face, Elucia reminds us, is our perception that there *is* an obstacle.

What seems to be unfounded fear many times is based on past events. We were scolded or punished as children, and this past prevents us from moving forward now. We tend to carry past hurts as if doing so will protect us from being hurt again—but of course it doesn't. It only keeps us from trying, from putting ourselves out there so we can learn and grow and experience. I've worked with so many people who are afraid of furthering their education because an elementary school teacher embarrassed them in front of the class and other people who will not even try to have a healthy relationship because they are afraid of making mistakes. When we can acknowledge the hurt behind our fears, then we can move beyond both. Fear, Elucia tells us in Chapter 3, *divides* us from the Divine. When we come together in kindness and compassion, we return to the energy of the Divine and realize there is nothing to fear.

It is a message seemingly as old as the angels themselves ... and as timely now as ever. "Be not afraid"—so prevalent in the writings of the Old Testament—has become the universal mantra of our modern times, times in which fear seems to abound. Spiritual leaders from Pope John Paul II, who repeated these words to inaugurate his papacy in 1978, to the fourteenth Dalai Lama, who reminds us that fear and suspicion are among the greatest obstacles to inner peace and happiness, reiterate this message of encouragement and strength. "We can let the circumstances of our lives harden us so that we become increasingly resentful and afraid, or we can let them soften us and make us kinder and more open to what scares us," writes Buddhist nun Pema Chodron in her book *The Places That Scare You: A Guide to Fearlessness in Difficult Times.*

In the Light: Calming Your Inner Child

You have something to do, but you are afraid to do it. You know there is nothing that can seriously hurt you, yet you are afraid. What can you do to dispel your fear? Sit with it. Go into the quiet. Ask yourself,

"How old do I feel?" Be honest. Visualize what happened with you or to you at that age. Talk to the child in the visualization and ask the child what it is that would allow him or her to feel safe. Now visualize yourself giving the child what he or she needs. How do you feel after going through it? To further explore and understand this fear and the circumstances responsible for it, write about it in your journal.

Unexpected Angels

I grew up in Brooklyn, New York, in the midst of ethnic and cultural diversity. As I came into my own as an artist, I explored many of these experiences through my paintings and drawings. The Chapel Gallery displayed one of these explorations, my series *City Folks,* which was a collection of larger-than-life portraits of inner-city people that was eight years in the making. It never occurred to me that the experiences commonplace for me, which I presented in this series, might cause other people to feel frightened or threatened. Yet I heard from one woman who was absolutely terrified when she first went into the exhibit and saw my paintings of inner city people. But she returned to the exhibit each day during the month it was there, and, one by one, developed relationships with the paintings.

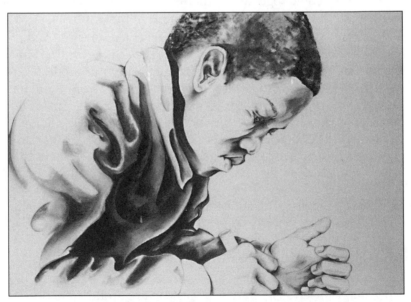

Rita's drawing, Working with a Marker.

By the end of the exhibit's run, she felt she knew each work as a friend and was entirely comfortable with the exhibit. I always viewed this as the angels working through my creative energy to reach people who otherwise would not confront and overcome their fears. Sometimes it takes unconventional ways for us to shake loose the perceptions we have of people who are different from us, perceptions that block us and prevent us from remembering that we are all connected through the divine. These paintings—and the people who are in them—are angels for the people who see and explore them as works of art and as connections to their own lives. Where in your life do you find similar kinds of connections?

Someone to Lean On

"You're such an angel!" How often do we say that to our really good friends—those wonderful people who answer the phone at 2 in the morning and let us talk through a rough day at work, the breakup of a relationship, or even a bad dream? These are the people in our lives who go above and beyond to touch us in ways that make us feel we're worthwhile. Our worth is something we question often, and our friends provide the validation that our lives are valued and have value. Our friends love us despite our imperfections. They are our chosen families, the people we *want* to be with in good times and bad. Our friends not only encourage us when we're doing something really wonderful but also let us know when we're doing something really wrong. They give us the love, the guidance, and the ear, as with the archangel Gabriel, to pour our troubles into.

Gabriel, you remember, is the angel, who in Christian, Judaic, and Islamic traditions, sits at the left hand of God with trumpet—the symbol of communication—in hand. He has God's ear, so to speak, and God has his. The divine and the angel sit in communion with one another, each knowing the other is there. This communion with the divine is present for each one of us, too. The energy of Gabriel is what we look for in a confidante when we need to convey our messages to the divine.

Who are the people, the friends, in your life who give you similar safe haven? Who are the friends who can give you the space to be with your thoughts and still give you the comfort of their company? These are the people who come in and help us overcome our own fears, the fears that block our paths and keep us from becoming our full selves. They are there to help us meet the challenges of significant life-altering events such as serious illness and loss or to celebrate with us our joys and successes.

They are there simply to be with us when we don't want to be alone, quiet when we don't want to talk, comforting when we need a hug or a shoulder to cry on. They are there for us; they are angels in our lives. And remember, you are also an angel in the lives of your friends because you, in turn, listen, encourage, and comfort them as they need for you to do.

Light Works: The Lights of Your Life

Candles have significance in many spiritual practices because they bring light and energy. Why not make your own candles to honor and celebrate the angels in your life? You can buy wicks and wax for making candles at most crafts stores. Other materials you need include a stove, double boiler pan (or one larger and one smaller pan if you don't have a double boiler), cooking or candy thermometer, thin stick for stirring (a chopstick works well), containers for your candles, scented oils, and candle coloring or food coloring if you desire. Use glass or metal for container candles or small cartons (such as milk cartons) as molds from which you will remove the candle after it is set.

1. Place wicks in the candle containers or molds, with the metal base in the center and the wick as upright as possible. Don't worry, you'll have an opportunity to adjust the wick as the wax begins to harden. Or you can fasten the wick to the bottom of the container with a small piece of tape to help hold it in place. Leave the wick 2 or 3 inches longer than the top of the container so you can manipulate the wick as the candle sets; you can trim it when the candle is hard.

2. Heat water in the bottom of the double boiler, and place broken chunks of wax in the top. As the wax begins to melt, monitor the temperature with the thermometer. When the temperature reaches 160°F, the wax should be completely melted. If you do not have a thermometer, the wax is hot enough when all the solid pieces have melted to liquid.

   Caution: Hot wax can burn! Do not leave the melting wax unattended, and remove it from the heat as soon as it becomes liquid or reaches 160°F.

3. If you want to use fragrances and coloring, add them to the melted wax and stir them in by using the stick. After the coloring and scent have been thoroughly mixed in, you can remove the wax from the heat.

4. Slowly pour the liquid wax into the containers or molds, using the wick as a guide to pour the wax down. Be sure the top of the wick stays above the wax.

5. As the wax begins to cool and harden, adjust the wick so it is in the center of the candle. When the top of the candle around the wick hardens into a depression, add more melted wax to bring the candle's top level again.

6. Allow the candle to cool and harden completely. If you used molds, pull them away when the wax is hard but still warm.

Light your finished candles to honor the angels in your life, and use them when you meditate or pray. Feel the energy and warmth of the flame, and notice the strength of the candle's light. If you like, dedicate each candle to a particular angel or to a loved one. The tradition of burning candles in dedication or devotion extends across belief systems and often draws us together in solidarity, as in prayer vigils when the tiny flames of each individual's candles merge to become a powerful and moving symbol—and reality—of light in the deepest darkness.

And a final note of caution: Be safe! Make sure to burn your candles only when you are present.

Under Wing

In our lives, we often have mentors and supporters who guide us and open doors to opportunities. These people take us under their wings to shelter us and at the same time teach us, like a mother duck teaching her young to swim—or an angel providing safe harbor. Maybe when you were young, a scout leader or youth program director provided productive ways for you to spend your time. Perhaps you had teachers who encouraged you and fostered your desire to learn. And in your career, maybe you have a boss or someone established who took you under his or her wing to strengthen your abilities and smooth your rough edges.

These are the people who can see your potential and choose to help you develop it, without any self-interest or hidden agendas of their own. Certainly in our jobs and professions, few of us could be where we are without these people. They are our angels; they help us give flight to our dreams and aspirations. And sometimes they help us see the right direction along our lifepaths when we are blind to it.

When I first entered the Spiritualist Church, I encountered a medium named Alice who approached me, introduced herself, and said, "Rita, you're going to be a spirit artist." At the time, that was not what I envisioned my path to be and I said, " no way, no how. That's not my calling." But Alice persisted. Every time she saw me, which was at least once a week, she insisted I would be a spirit artist. This just was not what I wanted to hear; my vision of myself was that of a painter and that was all I wanted to do. Several times Alice invited me to the mediumship classes she was teaching. Each time I politely declined. She kept insisting and I kept resisting until finally she wore me down and I went to one of her classes.

The experience was overwhelming. As soon as the class got underway, I began receiving images of those coming in from the higher side and I started to draw them. When the drawings were complete, the people in the class recognized the images I had drawn. I was astounded. And I recognized even before that first class was over that Alice was right; part of my path was to be a spirit artist. I could no longer deny it. I began to incorporate spirit drawing into my mediumship, and within a short time, it became the key element of my spiritual work.

Many of us find ourselves working in one area to support our love of another interest. Who do you know who paints, takes photographs, does fine woodworking, writes poetry or fiction, sculpts, plays an instrument, or sings in a band? So many people have "day jobs" to pay the bills and support the interests that give them joy and fulfillment. Some people are blessed to have achieved a level of success in their areas of interest that they can turn to their avocations full-time. Someone comes across their work and opens doors, and their life takes a major turn. Nearly every person who has achieved prominence has had such an angel (and usually several such angels) in his or her life. Even the Renaissance masters who created the striking works of art that define the image of angels in Western culture got a helping hand when they were starting out on their paths as artists. Bernini, Botticelli, and Caravaggio (who you remember from Chapter 5) all attracted the attention of Church officials who commissioned them to do significant works. This gave them the freedom to focus on honing their creative abilities along with a vast and timeless audience for their art. Divine inspiration and divine intervention often travel hand-in-hand!

You are always nearer the divine and the true sources of your power than you think.
—John Burroughs (1837–1921), American essayist

Bright Lights

Think of the public figures who bring lessons and inspiration to the masses. The work of such actors as Tom Hanks and Denzel Washington presents the many facets of each of the characters these actors play and causes us to see even simple scenes and situations as multidimensional. Movie producer Steven Spielberg brings us thought-provoking entertainment that is sometimes funny, sometimes poignant, sometimes painful—but seldom allows us to leave the theater with the same notions and ideas we had while standing in line to buy popcorn and chocolate-covered peanuts.

Although we think of these people as stars for reasons that are other than ethereal, they are stars in the most celestial of meanings, too, because they cast a light we cannot help but see. They are contemporary angels bearing messages humankind needs to hear and presenting them in ways that we will pay attention to.

The strong performances of Oprah Winfrey and Whoopi Goldberg in the movie *The Color Purple,* for example, were an important inspiration for me when I was doing my *City Folks* series of paintings. The movie gave me a wide-angle view; the inner-city kids in my art classes and who became the subjects of my paintings gave me the close focus. Both elements were essential for the *City Folks* series to be authentic and to touch people. What movies or performances touch you and bring you inspiration? What about them appeals to you? What have you done to act on the inspiration? If you've done nothing yet, what's holding you back?

Animal Companions

When I do readings for people, their pets often come in from the higher side or loved ones come in with their pets who were cherished companions when both were on the earth plane. Of course, this is enormously validating for people still on the earth plane as these are the details of life that can only be authentic. This also demonstrates how very attached we become to the dogs, cats, and other pets who are our animal friends. Our pets will stay by our sides no matter what—even when our human friends might decide they've had enough and need to take a break. Our pets stay with us when we're sick, when we're feeling down, and when we're otherwise alone. And our pets share the simple joys of life with such obvious enthusiasm. How excited does your dog get when you reach for the leash to go for a walk or pull out that favorite and lovingly chewed tennis ball for a game of chase the ball? How loud does your cat purr when you stroke her back, rub her chin, and give her a small tidbit of tuna or salmon?

When I did a spirit reading for Debbie McGillivray, she wanted me to draw her spirit guide. A spirit named Lin came in. Lin was an Asian herbalist, who showed herself crouched over a bowl as if grinding or mixing herbs, so that was how I drew her. At the time, Debbie has not told me much about herself. Several years later, I learned through a mutual acquaintance that Debbie was an animal communicator. At the time I did her spirit reading, Debbie was just beginning to use herbal therapies and homeopathy in her work with animals and was receiving images of medicinal plants that she knew were not coming from her own knowledge. These images often directed Debbie to nutritional imbalances and related problems in the animals, leading to remedies that restored them to health. The direction was coming from Lin, a spirit guide who came to help Debbie with what was then a new focus in her work with animals. Debbie now calls on Lin with intent whenever she is working with an animal she feels has nutritional problems or issues.

As an interesting footnote to this story: The same week my friend told me that Debbie was an animal communicator, book producer Lee Ann Chearney of Amaranth called me to ask if I knew anyone who could work on a book about communicating with animals. Of course by then I did, so I passed on Debbie's name. Debbie became co-author with Eve Adamson of *The Complete Idiot's Guide to Pet Psychic Communication* (Alpha Books, 2004). Talk about the divine order of the Universe!

Rita's drawing of spirit guide Lin the Asian herbalist.

Light Works: A Thank You Card

When someone does something special for us, we like to show our appreciation and gratitude. So often we go into greeting card stores looking for just the right card for someone in our life who has helped us. It can't be just any card; it has to be as special as the person we're sending it to. It has to be exactly what we're trying to say with an accompanying image that will express the right message of gratitude to this very special person. How often do you find such a card? If you're like me, not very often! So do what I do? I make my own, and you can, too, easily.

You don't have to be a writer or an artist to make your card. Giving thanks is about speaking from your heart. Who is the person you want to thank? Why do you want to thank this person? Go into meditation and ask your guides and angels for the perfect words to express your gratitude, then ask them for the image to go on the front of the card. There's your card! Have fun and create.

Continuing the Work

Knowledge does not die when the body does. Do you think Chopin came into this world to play a few tunes on the piano and then disappear forever? Of course not! No doubt Chopin is as busy on the higher side as he was on the earth plane, giving guidance and inspiration to who knows how many talented and aspiring musicians. The Universe is an endlessly generous energy; those who excel in their realms remain accessible as spirit guides to help those whose lifepaths might travel similar directions or those who ask for their help. You can ask for guidance from those who have passed to the higher side whose expertise might help you in your life. Each morning when I start my day, I ask the master artists who are among my spirit guides to help me do the best work I can do throughout the day.

It's not just the famous who continue their work from the higher side. My dear friend Duffy, a firefighter and a Spiritualist, passed to spirit. He and I had always joked about his helping me in the church. After he passed, I felt his presence one day while I was in my car. I asked him, "So are you going to help me now?" He said, "I'm going to be helping the young firefighters from spirit." At the time I didn't understand what he meant. But exactly one year later, on September 11, 2001, terrorists attacked the World Trade Center in New York City. Hundreds of firefighters lost their lives.

It wasn't easy to lose Duffy as a friend on the earth plane; it isn't ever easy to lose a loved one. But I was thrilled when I realized what that message was all about. He was in fact doing very important work from the higher side. We can do something creative in that person's memory to say thank you. We are giving a gift to the person's spirit. and transforming the pain we feel into joy we can share. You've heard the axiom, "What goes around comes around." That's what it's all about! People help you; you help other people. Think of the people you know in your life who touch and change the lives of others. We help and give to each other as angels.

The first beginnings of things cannot be distinguished by the eye.
—Titus Lucretius Carus (98–55 B.C.), Roman poet

In the Light: "And Now I'd Like to Thank ..."

The events that happen to you as your lifepath unfolds are not just the manifestations of Divine order. *You* make choices and decisions that guide your journey. The angels—earthly and ethereal—who help you do so because in some way you have asked for their help, either consciously or through your higher self. Giving thanks for this help is very important; we need to give as well as receive acknowledgment and appreciation for the healing efforts that make such a difference in our lives.

Shakespeare said that all of life is a stage. We've seen so many award shows and heard the acceptance speeches of gratitude for all the help the recipient has received. For a few moments, imagine that your life is a screenplay and you've just won the Academy Award. What would you say in your acceptance speech? Write a short speech, remembering that time is closely being watched, to thank the angels in your life who have helped make you the person you are. Then stand up and read your speech out loud as if you were giving it at the awards ceremony (although no one else needs to hear it unless you want to share it).

The State of Grace

Our angel card word for this chapter is *grace,* which is one of my favorite words. When you are in a state of grace, you feel a sense of oneness and of calmness. You feel centered and one with the Divine, one with the Universe. The energy of your solar plexus, the seat of your will or the "I will" part of you, is peaceful and without stress. When you are in a state of grace, you are not worried about being protected or being safe; you just have a knowledge that it is so. How do you acquire grace? By letting go of fear and by learning to trust the Divine. This is an essential aspect of personal growth and evolution. When we can trust in the Divine and in each other, we have no reason to fear and worry. In a state of grace, we can follow our lifepaths with confidence, knowing we are journeying in the right direction. Grace is incredibly powerful and empowering.

Light Works: Chapter 6 Angel Card

This chapter's angel card word is *Grace.* What does it mean to be in a state of grace? There is a calmness, a peacefulness, and a thankfulness for being alive and being one with the Divine. What does that look like? Imagine in color and movement, or in images you find in photographs and magazine pictures, what it means to be in grace. With your guides and angels, design your angel card for *Grace.*

Highest and Best: Opening Your Throat Chakra

We need to speak but we're afraid, so we close the throat chakra. No expressions come from us; all stays bottled within. What do we need to say, and will anyone hear us? There are times when we feel so alone or that we need to talk but the person we need to talk to isn't there for us. Sometimes the person has already passed, but even if so, it's not too late. The fear we hold on to from the past can inhibit our lives in the present. We must work to open the throat so we can speak our truth.

The fifth chakra, the throat chakra, is the chakra of communication. When it becomes blocked, not only do we have difficulty speaking our truth, but we are prone to colds, sore throats, stiff necks, and thyroid or hearing problems, too. We again can ask our guides, loved ones, and angels to help us. We can use turquoise or visualize the color bright blue and chant "Ham" to help open the throat chakra. Here's how:

1. Sit in a meditative pose such as lotus or cross-legged. If this is not possible, sit upright in a chair with your back as straight as possible. Take a deep breath, pulled in from your diaphragm.

2. As you allow your diaphragm to slowly push the breath back out, allow your vocal cords to form the sound "*Ham.*" Let the sound extend for the full length of the exhalation.

3. Repeat this exercise until you feel the strain and stress leave your throat and hear the sound of your voice become calm and steady. I like to ask Kwan Yin, the motherly goddess of compassion, to guide my energy.

Yoga's fish posture also can help open the throat chakra. Here's how to do this posture:

1. Lie on your back on the floor (put down a yoga mat or rug if you like) with your legs stretched out and your feet together. This is called corpse pose in yoga.

2. Take three deep, cleansing breaths in through your nose and out through your mouth. Take the first breath in to clear your body, then slowly release the breath. Take the second breath to open your mind, and take a third breath to free your spirit.

3. Slide your arms under your back with your palms turned down under your buttocks. Be sure your elbows are pressed toward the floor and not out.

4. Flex your heels and press them away from your hips.

5. Push down on your elbows and raise your chest, resting your weight on your elbows. This raises your whole upper body off the floor.

6. Carefully allow your head to bend backward until the crown (top) touches the floor. This arches your back and stretches your neck, opening your throat chakra.

7. With your buttocks ("sit bones") pressing against the floor to hold some of your weight, lower your back onto your elbows. Carefully raise your head to stay in line with your body.

8. Relax and breathe in, slowly and deeply from your diaphragm, the benefits of this posture.

9. When you feel you have completed these benefits, let your body return to how it was in step 1 (corpse pose).

10. Remaining in corpse pose, close your eyes and allow your mind to visualize what it needs to incorporate the energy of this pose into your being. Envision it as so.

You are, of course, always in communication with your angels and spirit guides—it's just that sometimes you don't recognize it! Awareness brings you to grace (our angel card word for this chapter) and compassion, helping you focus your efforts and your energy to bring peace and joy to yourself and to others. You open yourself to the possibilities that surround you, and to the many gifts that others bring to your life.

Part 3

Learning From Your Angels: Be Not Afraid

Each of us has lessons to learn in this life. Our souls agree to learn these lessons; they are part of our reason for being here. Sometimes our lessons come in the forms of what feel like overwhelming challenges. Our angels are here to help us learn and evolve. All we have to do is ask for their guidance and pay attention to their responses. But what about when you ask for something but don't get it? Sometimes what we ask for isn't what we really need to move along our paths.

In the 1947 movie *The Bishop's Wife*, the angel Dudley (played by Cary Grant) tells Bishop Henry Brougham (played by David Niven) that he's leaving.

"You've gotten what you prayed for," Dudley tells the bishop.

"But I prayed for a cathedral!" Henry protests.

"No. You were praying for guidance. That's been given to you," Dudley replies.

When you form your request or question with purity of intent, you receive what you need ... even if it's not what you think you are asking for.

Sometimes, Henry, angels must rush in where fools fear to tread.
—Dudley the Angel (played by Cary Grant) in *The Bishop's Wife* (1947)

Chapter 7

Devils in Angel Clothes: Troublemakers Are Gifts

We all have devils—inner and outer—in our lives. In human terms, we label people "devils" who manage to challenge us no matter what the circumstances, who sometimes seem to enjoy getting us riled up for no good reason, or who seem to want to test us in all the wrong ways. Maybe your devil is a boss, an ex, or a demanding (unfair!) teacher or parent; maybe your devil is a willful child, a willful grandparent, or a betraying best friend .... The possibilities are as endless as the nature of human relations. In one way or another, these devils might be the people closest to us, depending on us as we depend on them, yet they behave in such devilishly outrageous ways that we want to run, not walk, away. How can we look at the gifts these seemingly darker angels bring us? And is it worth our trouble to try?

Confronting our devils with love and compassion is a definite challenge. But seeing our devils as the highest angelic gift can lead us to expanded personal awareness and evolution. Whether you *ever* have a good or transformed relationship with your demons—no matter if their devilish source is from within or from without—after a while, in the right light, you might be able to begin to see a devil's higher purpose and recognize this person, situation, or energy for the *good* in your life, not just the trouble or destructive influence it exerts. Sometimes you might even find that *you* are your own devil who creates challenges for yourself as well as for others!

In the Light: Give Yourself Healing Energy

When the devils in our lives are challenging us, often we find it difficult to connect to the calm and inner Divine center that gives us strength. We struggle to find the empowerment we need to transform these demons, to welcome the provocations they drop at our feet. We feel distanced from the angels, on the earth plane and on the higher side, who can help us slay our dragons. At such times we can soothe ourselves by sending self-healing chakra energy through aromatherapy. When we can calm ourselves we can see more clearly.

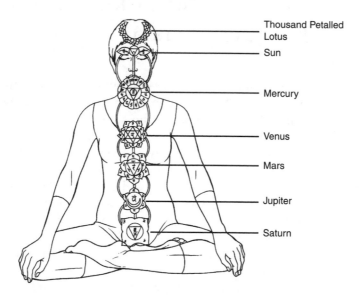

Thousand Petalled Lotus

Sun

Mercury

Venus

Mars

Jupiter

Saturn

The seven chakras are energy centers that can help connect us to the Spirit realm.

Essential oils convey the energies of the substances that comprise them. You can put a few drops of the appropriate essential oils in an aromatherapy diffuser, in the melted wax of a burning candle (take care not to get the oil on the wick), or on a piece of cotton that you then place on a cool light bulb. When you turn on the light, the oil dissipates into the air as the bulb warms. You can also put a few drops of essential oil into a tub of warm water and enjoy a soothing, healing bath (although do not put essential oils directly on your skin, as they can create irritation). You can find essential oils and aromatherapy diffusers at health stores and shops that specialize in items related to the esoteric arts.

If you like, work with the chakra energies for a week, one day for each chakra; or for seven weeks, one week for each chakra; or even seven months, one month for each chakra (some devils can be stubborn!). You will learn more in Chapter 8 about using chakra energy to connect to the higher realm and converse with your angels, but for now, choose the chakra energy most needed to help you relax and center yourself as you call to the Divine:

- **Root chakra:** Use ylang ylang, myrrh, patchouli, or sandalwood essential oil. Visualize the color red, and state the affirmation, I feel safe in the physical world. I have vitality, courage, and confidence.

- **Sacral chakra:** Use orange, jasmine, or geranium essential oil. Visualize the color orange, and state the affirmation, I am happy and resourceful. I am ambitious without sacrificing those I love. My sensuality flows.

- **Solar plexus chakra:** Use juniper, rosemary, lemon, or marjoram essential oil. Visualize the color yellow, and state the affirmation, I am wise and aware. I live life to the fullest and am worthy of receiving.

- **Heart chakra:** Use eucalyptus, pine, or rosewood essential oil. Visualize the color green, and state the affirmation, I can love unconditionally and maintain self-control. I am harmonious with all those around me and with myself.
  Visualize pink instead of green to stimulate the heart chakra for universal love.

- **Throat chakra:** Use chamomile, sage, or lemongrass essential oil. Visualize the color blue, and state the affirmation, I communicate holistically. I express myself freely and openly and I am heard.

- **Third eye chakra:** Use lavender, peppermint, or clary sage essential oil. Visualize the color indigo, and state the affirmation, I connect with my unconscious, mystical self. I am opened to inner vision and spiritual truth.

- **Crown chakra:** Use frankincense, myrrh, or angelica essential oil. Visualize the color violet, and state the affirmation, I am inspired. I am connected with the universe. I am one with the Divine.

The serpent disappears in a blinding sunburst of radiance and in its place stands an angel resplendent and shining, golden garments with great scarlet wings that spread from one corner of the heavens to the other.
—Manly P. Hall (1901–1990), American scholar of the esoteric

Of Demons and Devils

So what do *devils* look like? Through the history of humankind, there are nearly as many representations of devils as of angels. Early mythologies feature devils as characters of mischief and fun, a bit irresponsible in the quest for a good time but otherwise generally not evil or even all that malicious in their intentions. Often demons were archetypes representing without judgment, as archetypes do, the various dimensions of human existence such as greed or lust.

Our modern word *demon,* which we use as a synonym for "devil," comes from the ancient Greek *daemon,* which simply meant "spirit." The image of the devil as a horned-man figure with cloven hooves harkens to Pan, the Greek god of good times. Such representation carries forward in other mythologies in which this devil is merely the spirit of the woods, the ultimate mountain man (or woman, though in different form, of course). In ancient Hindu mythology, devilish nymphs called *apsara* sang to the monks from the treetops in an effort to lure them into carnal pleasures. The word *devil* arises from the ancient Hebrew word for "adversary," later adopted into the Greek (one of the early languages of education and culture) as *diabolos,* which later came to mean "one who slanders." The convergence of demon and devil as the same concept and entity signals the meeting of Western and Eastern cultures.

Over time, devils and demons came to represent the less-pleasant dimensions of life. Seventeenth-century sailors spoke with great dread of drawing lots to do that which was "between the devil and the deep blue sea" and of having "the devil to pay and no pitch hot." Both phrases referred to the sometimes necessary and always hazardous duty of water-proofing with hot pitch the seam between the planks of a wooden sailing ship's hull where they rode just above the water line. Even today we hear these phrases in reference to situations where the only options are equally arduous or unpleasant (although not usually as dangerous as sealing the devil). And perhaps you've heard a grandparent say, "I had a devil of a time ..." Although today we automatically assign a sense of difficulty to this phrase, in its origin, it meant having a good time!

How many of these other "devil phrases" do you know:

- **Devil's advocate.** Common today as a term identifying someone who takes an opposite view for no reason other than to instigate debate, the *Advocatus Diaboli* was the official appointed by the Roman Catholic Church to present arguments opposing a proposed canonization.

- **Pull the devil by the tail.** A circumstance of continuous struggle and adversity.

- **Devil dog.** A half-admiring, half-disparaging moniker German soldiers in World War I applied to U.S. Marines in reference to the tenacity and fierce fighting of the 4th Brigade.

- **The devil's bedpost.** The 4 of Clubs in a deck of playing cards.

- **Speak of the devil, and you'll soon see his horns.** I prefer the flip side of this adage: Speak of an angel, and you'll feel the wind of wings!

The Seductive Powers of Your Devils

The historical blend of devilish fun and potential for destruction reveal how seductive the devil can be. The devil seduces by tempting, cajoling, provoking, teasing, or meddling—whatever works! Maybe you're seduced into obtaining your creative talent the "easy" way by selling your soul at the crossroads like guitarist Robert Johnson. Or maybe, when you're looking for love, you'd line up 10 women or men and pick the potential partner who'd be the most "trouble" (that is, the devil of the group). When the devil tempts, you often end up looking at your Jungian shadow side, that dark twin psychoanalyst Carl Jung described who balances the light in each of us, almost as dark yin energy balances bright yang energy.

But seduction isn't always *easy*, and we might find our desire thwarted in the most devilishly unexpected ways. When this happens, we need to take a second look at the demons in our lives; they might do more than bedevil us ... they might jump-start us out of stagnant thinking or prompt us to redirect certain aspects of our lives such as a career or relationship, as was the case with Ramon.

The reason Milton wrote in fetters when he wrote of Angels and God, and at liberty when of Devils and Hell, is because he was a true poet and of the Devil's party without knowing it.
—William Blake (1757–1827), British poet and artist

After years of working in pay-the-bills kinds of jobs, Ramon went back to school to study what had interested him all his life: energy healing. He began his studies with great enthusiasm (doing what you love should be *easy*, right?) but soon found that his instructor took devilish pleasure playing mind games with his students. In such a discouraging environment, student after student dropped out, disillusioned and demoralized. Ramon, too, became frustrated, but he did not want to slink back to the seduction of a weekly paycheck if it meant working a job he didn't love.

So did that mean he should stick it out with a teacher he didn't like who might poison his very interest in energy healing? Ramon switched his enrollment to an acupuncture program that included classes in polarity therapy. The new instructors were encouraging and supportive, and Ramon loved the program's integration of therapeutic approaches, which were very unique at the time. After graduating, Ramon opened a clinic, which flourished.

We can view Ramon's first discouraging instructor as a devilish wake-up call to persevere. When you look at your own life, who (or what) are the devils you wrestle with to find innovative ways to accomplish your goals?

Rita's The Fight; *we wrestle our demons.*

In the Light: One with the Divine

As in the unified duality of yin and yang, dark and light are expressions of the Divine whole. Once upon a time, Christian angel lore tells us, the angels all lived together in peace and harmony. Each angel had a role and responsibility in the heavenly order, and most embraced theirs with joy and integrity. There was a little jostling and jockeying for favor with God, of course, because the angels, although not human and, thus, not subject to human foibles, had their personalities and little quirks. Eventually, Lucifer picked one too many fights and was expelled from heaven. This was the time he became known as Satan, which means "adversary."

I once did a reading for a man who was having some problems in his life. He kept referring to the angel Lucifer—not to Lucifer the devil but to Lucifer the angel. After he left, I started thinking about this rather intriguing turn on common perception. I realized the ability to find the Divine within, the light in darkness, is what helps us turn around and change direction in our lives.

Who in your life strikes fear and loathing in your heart when you hear their name or see them coming toward you? Write this person's name, then write the reasons you feel fear or anger when you think of the person:

_____ makes me feel angry or afraid because _____
_____
_____.

Now, change the person's name to "The Light" and read the reasons you wrote. How does this change how you feel? It becomes very interesting!

Sometimes our reluctance to see the light and the dark *both* as part of the Divine and as part of the oneness prevents us from seeing the angelic potential of our darkest devils. When you identify the person who makes you feel angry or afraid, what issues surrounding this person come up in you? Like the archetype represented by the Major Arcana card The Devil (no matter how it's depicted in any Tarot deck), we see our fears bind us and blindside us so we are unable to see the whole picture, to see the light that balances the dark. Once we can confront our fears, we can free ourselves from the darkness and heal our lives in the light. We remember we are one with the Divine, and the Divine is one with us.

Devilish Challenges

Years ago, I had an employer who was a tough man. He really liked pushing people's buttons to see how much he had to dish out to break them down. This person enjoyed public humiliation and did things to embarrass people, but somehow during the 15 years I worked for him, I had managed to skirt around this. It took a long time for my boss to push me to my bottom line, but when I got there, that was it. I left the job. That difficult person actually led me to my work with troubled adolescents and the *City Folks* paintings. Dark balancing light? Yes, definitely!

The obvious devils in our lives often take the form of other people. They are real people such as my former boss or Ramon's teacher, although often these devil-people represent issues much deeper than the circumstances at hand. Like the deities of ancient cultures, they stand as archetypes for particular aspects or dimensions of life. Often we can gain tremendous insight and personal growth when we take the time and effort to understand our devils and the roles they play in our lives. We can learn important lessons from difficult and even ugly situations. Those who are our devils in these situations often have their own lessons to learn, as well—something we often forget when we're experiencing their devilish ways ....

This is not to say, however, that we must stick around to see what we need to learn from abusive or harmful situations or figure out how someone who is abusive is helping us grow. When a situation or person is abusive, get out! Leave, seek professional assistance, or do whatever it takes to remove yourself from harm's way. And of course, not all our lessons are difficult to the extent of being painful. Many of life's lessons are humorous and fun—especially, it seems, when they're over and we can look back on them and laugh.

"The Devil Made Me Do It"

Comedian Flip Wilson, popular in the 1970s, had a stage character named Josephine whose favorite line was, "The devil made me do it!" How many times do we hear people say this or say it ourselves (or at least think it even if we don't say it out loud)? It seems only human nature that we tend to blame others instead of taking responsibility for our own actions. Sometimes we can't see that the responsibility belongs to us, and sometimes even when we do, we are reluctant to admit that it does. For example, you become a doctor because your parents wanted you to be one, or you move across the country because your spouse needed to be happy. Or you could become an electrician instead of a musician because a steady paycheck is better than the unpredictability of following the creative muse, or you give up working and all your independent interests because that's what a mother should do for a child's care and happiness. However, if your motivation for doing these things does not come from your true core being, then ... well ... why *not* blame others for the ways your own discomfort can and *will* devilishly manifest through your own actions and words?

These words have turn'd my hate to love,
And I forgive and quite forget old faults.
—William Shakespeare (1564–1616), playwright

Other people in our lives, often in the role of our devils, motivate and even compel us to evaluate our lives and circumstances. Often these confrontations come when things are not going so well, although this doesn't have to be the case. Sometimes everything seems to be going just fine, yet there's that undercurrent of doubt or discomfort that tugs at us. *It's just my insecurity,* you might be able to tell yourself for a while. But the longer it takes you to get the message, the more outside forces will come to bear on opening your eyes to the need for change, until eventually you encounter a "devil" who forces that undercurrent to the surface of your awareness where you can no longer ignore it or pretend it does not exist. These devils can be agents—or in truth, angels—of change in our lives.

Do these angelic agents *make* us change? No, of course they don't. For each of us, the choice to change is ours and ours alone, no matter how intense or persistent outside influences become. We might feel powerless to do anything else, perhaps because of the influence of others in our lives or because there appear to be no other options. This is a time to stop for a moment, think, and get a little perspective. Then we can make our own choices. We can act rather than react. Nobody will come in and do this for you, not even your angels. Your angels will guide you and help you, but they won't come in to act for you. You have to take responsibility for yourself, your decisions, your actions, and your life.

In the Light: Facilitators for Change

Who are the devilish angels who push and prod and nag and pester you? Who are your agents of change, those who force you to examine your decisions and choices?

Think of a time in your life when you received a message to make a change or go in a different direction. What was the circumstance?

_____

_____

_____

Who was the person who became a motivator or facilitator for change?

_____

_____

_____

How did you respond to this person's involvement?

_____

_____

_____

What constraints did you feel limited your choices and course of action?

_____

_____

_____

Did you take the path of change that was presenting itself to you? Why or why not?

_____

_____

_____

What happened?

_____

_____

_____

Were you pleased or satisfied with the outcome? Why or why not?

_____

_____

_____

If you could go back to this same situation now, what would you do differently and why?

_____

_____

_____

When You Are the Devil

Robert was promoted to supervisor after working in his department for five years. His co-workers expressed strong confidence in his knowledge and ability to get along with people, and his manager felt Robert would make an excellent supervisor. But three months after his promotion, 6 of the department's 10 staff had quit or transferred to other departments. Robert, the employees said during their exit interviews, was an impossible supervisor who did not tolerate methods different from his own. Robert was stunned when his manager called him in for counseling. "I thought that's why you promoted me!" Robert said. "Sure, I have high standards, but I never expect more from my staff than I would do myself!"

Sometimes we, like Robert, become the devils in the lives of other people. We pressure and influence others in ways that they find objectionable or unpleasant. Under the best of circumstances, we are genuine in our motivations to push for the best rather than acting from malicious intent. Sometimes we're lucky enough that a friend or co-worker takes us aside and says to us in the kindest of ways, "Are you nuts?!" Other times, we so alienate those around us that they simply step aside and wait for us to crash of our own volition.

As hard as these lessons are, they are their own angelic gifts delivered to us on gossamer wings even as we stand there dressed up in our red devil suits! And the gift we learn from is found not in how hard and fast we fall from heaven to hell through our devilish behavior (intended or unintended), but how quickly we pick ourselves back up and whether (and how) we accept responsibility and move toward positive change for ourselves and those we've bedeviled.

Sometimes we become the devils in our *own* lives. We might engage in compulsive or self-destructive behaviors. (We commonly refer to overcoming addiction as a process of wrestling with our demons.) We might confuse *won't* for *can't*, erecting our own roadblocks to success and happiness. We might follow the same patterns of behavior over and over and over, knowing even as we embark on yet another round of the same routine that we've been there, done that ... and we're falling for that same old devil seduction *again*.

Outer Devil, Inner Angel

For one of my clinical psychology internships, I worked as a counselor in a center for adolescent girls, in a residential unit for girls who had gotten in trouble with the law. In addition to the clinical counseling and case-management responsibilities of my internship, I also was running an art program for these girls. As I was watching them work on their projects one day, I was struck by the beauty of their creations and the appearance of them all so focused and intent on manifesting the inspiration within them. I said to them, "You all are angels."

Of course that inspired a lot of chuckling and commentary, because all these girls were at the center because they'd broken the law. Many came from difficult life situations. Certainly they did not think of themselves as angels. But I told them, "You all are angels on the inside. You just have a whole lot of stuff on the outside that keeps you from getting in touch with that inner angel."

None of them said much at the time, but a few weeks later, when we started planning our unit's holiday decorations, clearly all the girls had angels on their minds. I helped them make angels in art class, and we used them to decorate the unit's Christmas tree for the annual holiday celebration and contest. The girls loved their tree so much they decided to turn their entire unit into heaven. We made clouds out of fluffy fabric and hung them from the walls. We made more angels and put them on the walls as well as and more decorations from pipe cleaners and tissue paper. Then each girl wrapped a white bed sheet around herself to make a dress—which was more of a challenge than it sounds as these girls were not permitted to have safety pins, needle and thread, or even paperclips. It was going to take some effort, but they put their ingenuity to work and looked truly like angels when they were finished. They even made halos and stars out of decorative wrapped ribbon. Then we turned on angelic holiday music and waited for the judges to come look at the decorations.

When the judges from the center's staff came through our unit, they were amazed at the vision that greeted them. The goodness inside those girls, for at least that one night, shone apparent on the outside as well. *They transformed themselves into angels.* They didn't just look like angels; they *became* the angels alive within each of them. The judges knew it, I knew it, and the girls knew it—we witnessed something magical. The night remains an absolute highlight in my life, and I still feel so blessed to have been part of the transformation.

Light Works: Chapter 7 Angel Card

This chapter's angel card word is *Forgiveness*. For this card, imagine that you are coming out of the darkness and transforming into a being of light. The darkness you are leaving feels heavy, and the light you are entering feels ethereal. Envision the colors, sounds, and movements this transformation incorporates. Using images that represent this transformation, create your angel card for *Forgiveness*.

Expectations and the Fall from Grace

So much of life is about expectations. We expect people to behave in certain ways. We expect situations to have certain outcomes. We expect devils to be devils and angels to be angels. Pure and simple. When events meet expectations, it's easy to feel joy, satisfaction, and completeness. But what happens when our expectations fail to materialize? What happens when our angels, the light beings of our hope and inspiration, fall?

Philip came into Karla's life at a time when Karla stood at a crossroads. Karla and her husband, George, had drifted into separate lives over the 20 years of their marriage. Karla felt unhappy and unsettled. This was not the life or the husband she'd envisioned for herself, and she didn't really understand how things had gotten so far out of hand. George seemed oblivious to the distance Karla felt and even, to Karla's amazement, content with things the way they were.

Karla met Philip at the fitness club. He was charming and appeared to be very caring. He seemed to be all that George was not, and Karla soon reached the point where she was ready to give up on her marriage and break up her family. But as her relationship with Philip intensified, Karla began to feel even more unsettled. She couldn't decide whether Philip (or George!) represented an angel or a devil, and she knew it was time for her to do some serious soul-searching.

One day as Karla was driving home from work, she looked up and saw that the sky had become the most glorious pastel colors. At the same time she heard a chorus of voices say, "Keep your marriage together. George is who you belong with." Karla felt a rush of clarity—about her life, about her marriage, about her expectations. When she got home, she went searching for her wedding ring, which she had stopped wearing when she met Philip. She put the ring back on her finger and made a commitment as she did so to make her marriage work.

It wasn't an easy pledge to keep. The marriage had reached the border of irretrievable strain, and Karla knew it would take much work to pull it back. But she knew the work would be worth it, so she turned her efforts to restoring the friendship and romance that had once drawn her and George together. At the times when it seemed an impossible challenge, Karla would step outside to look up at the sky. "You told me to keep my marriage together. Please help me do that." She would redeem this fallen angel, her marriage.

Karla's greatest challenge was to come to terms with her expectations—of George, of marriage, and of herself. This was not an easy challenge, as expectations are complex and many influences shape them. Teasing these influences apart and deciding which ones matter and which ones don't takes focus, self-honesty, and the willingness to make *internal* changes. Sure, Karla's motivators were external—her husband, her lover, and her marriage. But her expectations were very much internal, and only by exploring them at that level could she reach understanding.

If we really want to love we must learn how to forgive.
—Mother Teresa (1910–1997), Catholic nun, missionary, and 1979 Nobel Peace Prize Laureate

With effort (and a little help from our angels!) we can discover that our expectations have evolved from circumstances that are no longer valid. When Karla and George married, Karla looked to George to provide her with the "ideal" life even though she didn't know what that looked like. She did not expect that she would need to create her *own* ideal life, which she realized at this point of crisis in her marriage was not about George but about *herself*. Angels touched Karla's life; she recognized it and paid attention. The discovery empowered Karla to both accept and take responsibility for her choices in life, which was greatly freeing for her. And what about the outcome? Karla and George just celebrated their thirty-eighth anniversary, and both can say they are very happily married.

Light Works: Release Expectations

Expectations appear to be about others, but they're really about us, representing actions we want to see, words we want to hear, or behaviors we want to experience. When others fail to meet our expectations, when they become our fallen angels, we are disappointed, frustrated, and even angry. Unfulfilled expectations can keep us from enjoying the richness of life.

When we can release our expectations of others, we allow their inner angels, and our own, to emerge and soar again.

Do you have unmet expectations? If you do, maybe it's time to let them go. Here's how you might do that:

1. Go to a place where you can be undisturbed. Take pen and paper, a small metal or heat-proof glass bowl, a saucer or plate to hold the hot container, and matches or a lighter.

2. On a small piece of paper, write an expectation that was not fulfilled that is causing you to feel frustration, anger, or hurt. This is your fallen angel.

3. Meditate for a few minutes about this expectation. How did you come to form it? What happened (or did not happen) to leave it unfulfilled?

4. Place the paper in the heat-proof glass or metal bowl, and put the bowl on the saucer or plate. If you prefer, you can use a heavy ashtray or the fireplace instead. Light the paper with a match or lighter.

5. As you watch the paper burn, envision the expectation rising with the smoke to dissipate into the air, becoming molecules that are now free to form other creations.

6. Celebrate the release of the expectation, and ask your angels and guides to help you approach the person or situation with openness.

Making Amends: The Importance of Forgiveness

In the 2003 film adaptation of the stage play *Angels in America*, Roy Cohen (played by Al Pacino) is a tough, pragmatic lawyer proud of his reputation for ruthlessness. Getting the conviction that sent spy Ethel Rosenberg (played by Meryl Streep) to the electric chair was the turning point and crowning achievement of his career. Later in his life as he is dying of AIDS, Roy sees and converses with Ethel's ghost. She expresses little pity for his plight and pain, even taking a degree of satisfaction in observing his suffering. Yet at his death, she appears one final time in spirit to lead another character's recitation on the earth plane of the Yiskor, or Kaddish, prayer of mourning, over Roy's body:

Oseh shawlom bim'ro'mawv, hu ya'aseh shawlom, awleinu v'al kol yisroel v'imru: Amein.

He who makes peace in his heights, may he make peace, upon us and upon all Israel. Now respond: Amen.

It is a prayer of forgiveness and blessing, and the scene is one of the film's most moving for its intense and explicit message that we all are of the Divine and as such of each other—we are all darkness, we are all light. We say Kaddish *even for the devil* because we know we are each of us, at once devil and angel. We say this prayer in acknowledgment that we all come from and return to the Divine.

To say, "I forgive you" is empowering and freeing. The devil is more than simply difficult. The devils in our lives—in whatever form— sometimes create enormous challenges, disappointments, and pain. Those who are devils in your life have devils of their own. This doesn't make their actions right or even explain them. What is most important to understand and remember is that *the actions of your devils ultimately may have very little to do just with you.* Moreover, we cannot change the thoughts and actions of others. We can only let go and move forward; we must learn *to forgive the unforgivable.* When we bear grudges, we hold on to hurt and insecurity, chains that bind us to a past that is gone. To forgive is not to forget but to redeem, to release ourselves as well as those whom we believe hold us in chains.

Rita's drawing, I Forgive You.

In the Light: Your Prayer of Forgiveness

What devils in angel clothes are preventing you from moving forward in your life? What past experiences shadow you today, perhaps as vividly as if you live them again and again? Say a prayer of forgiveness, release them, then free yourself.

1. Go to your sacred place or a place you can be undisturbed and can say your prayer out loud.

2. As you say your prayer, feel and see the chains of this devil dissolving into dust that blows away in the wind, liberating you from this devil's hold and influence. You can use this simple prayer or create a prayer of your own:

> *Infinite Divine, I forgive _____ for actions and words that have been hurtful to me. Help me move forward in my life to use what I have learned for the highest and best, in love and at peace. Amen.*

Highest and Best: Forgive Yourself

Sometimes the devils that give us the greatest grief are the ones within us, the expectations and disappointments we carry about our own thoughts and actions. These inner devils can be more binding than any external devil; they often are harder for us to identify and, thus, to release.

But you can free yourself from these devils:

1. Go to your sacred space or a place where you will not be disturbed.

2. Take three cleansing breaths, in through your nose and out through your mouth. Take a deep breath in through your nose to clear your body, and release it. Take a second breath to open your mind and a third breath to free your spirit.

3. Recall an instance when you might have hurt someone's feelings or said something you wish you could take back. Perhaps there was an action that you wished never happened. Visualize that incident or those words.

4. Ask your guides and angels to come in and connect with you in this healing process of forgiveness.

5. Now visualize yourself asking the other person to forgive you. Express how you would really like the situation to turn out. Speak out loud, as if you were actually having a dialogue with the person.

6. Visualize the outcome as you would have it be now. See it as done.

7. Now turn to yourself and ask yourself for forgiveness. Most of the time we do not intentionally hurt other people. But even if an infliction is intentional, it still can be healed on the higher realms.

8. Visualize yourself being forgiven by you. See it as done.

9. Wrap yourself is a soft pink light of love and know that you deserve it.

Remember, we are all Divine. Every devilish darkness gives you an opportunity to grow in angelic light. Give yourself the time to do what you need to do so you can put this opportunity to good use. Ask your angels to help you stay centered within your Divine self. The choice is yours. Can you see your devil's angel clothes?

Chapter 8

Communicating With Your Angels

Have you ever been (or felt) lost and then discovered you've ended up exactly where you're supposed to be? We are most receptive to information coming in from our angels and the higher realm when we're least thinking about it This is one reason so many people receive Divine contact during those twilight moments between wake and sleep. Mundane tasks of repetition also open us naturally to the energy of the Universe and the messages it carries. Many thoughts and ideas with inspired intent come to me when I'm driving. For you, inspiration might come when you're taking a long, hot bath or shower; cooking or baking; gardening; or playing a sport. Some people call this ability being "in the zone"; but we know better: We are communicating with our angels!

As another example, have you ever wondered what to buy as a gift for someone or where you can get exactly what you need? Some of us are very busy people and shopping often becomes a major hassle. Whenever I need to purchase something, I ask my guides where I can get this item and get it at the best price. It always amazes me that with anything from ingredients for cooking to buying a car, I can find a sale or get a great deal by setting that intent and following the answer.

Sometimes people laugh at the notion of using this energy for something as simple as shopping or finding a parking spot. It's not so frivolous, though, when you think about it.

The more we work with angels, with Spirit, with our guides, and with the energies, the more our Divine intent becomes part of all we do. In this context, there is nothing too small—or too large—to ask for. Imagine what happens when you set the intent that you'll go right to *where you need to be!* That you'll have *what you need!* That you'll meet *the right people at the right times!* Obstacles are basically intention in reverse, and we create or are frustrated by them when we *don't* want to get somewhere. But as we learned in Chapter 7, devils can be angels, and everything we experience can lead us to Divine understanding.

We *all* can learn to harness a natural openness to use for intentional communication with our angels and the higher realm. Humanity possesses amazing abilities if only we, as individuals, put them to work. We have to remember to ask for what we need, set the intent, allow the answer to come, and move toward it. Our angels and spirit guides are waiting and ready to help us when we ask.

Far away there in the sunshine are my highest aspirations. I may not reach them, but I can look up and see their beauty, believe in them, and try to follow where they lead.

—Louisa May Alcott (1832–1888), American novelist

Know What You Are Asking For ...

In his early days of working with Spirit, my good friend and business mentor Bob Olson decided to "test" his spirit guide in what he thought was an innocuous enough way. Bob's wife had given him a watch as a gift. Although it was a very nice watch, it wasn't a watch Bob would have selected for himself, and he didn't particularly care for it (although he kept this to himself). After a week, the watch developed a problem. It would keep perfect time for a few hours, stop running for an hour or so, then start again. So Bob took the watch to a jeweler.

As Bob watched the jeweler fiddle around with the watch, he began to think, *I'd really like another watch instead.* So almost in a joking way, he started sending messages to his spirit guide asking that there be a problem of some sort with the watch that the jeweler could not resolve. Bob hoped maybe the jeweler would tell him the watch was defective and offer a replacement, so he started looking at the watches in the jeweler's display case, just in case his spirit guide came through for him.

Suddenly there was a loud cracking sound. Bob looked up to see the jeweler holding the watch's shattered crystal in his hand. "I've been doing this for 25 years and never broken a watch crystal," the jeweler said, shaking his head. "I don't know how this could have happened. I'm very sorry. This is an unusual crystal, and I don't have a replacement."

But Bob knew. Feeling somewhat sheepish, Bob accepted the jeweler's offer to choose a different watch from the case and vowed that from that moment on he would set his intentions with an integrity and honor worthy of their power. "What responsibility we have in setting our intentions for communicating with our angels and the higher realm!" Bob exclaimed when he told me about his experience.

Light Works: Chapter 8 Angel Card

This chapter's angel card word is *Intent*. The purpose of this angel card is to focus energy. The card needs a definite visual focal point, a place on the card that no matter where you look your eye always goes to that one specific spot. You can do this with direction (for example, circles within circles to draw the eye to the innermost dot); or you can do it with contrast (everything light or muted, and the focal point is dark or vice versa).Create a visual focal point using color and flow, and be inventive as you create your angel card for *Intent*.

Light Works: Setting Intent

Intent establishes our purpose when traveling the path of communication between the self-Spirit and angel, or higher Spirit. It is the embodiment of the highest and best. Intent represents our trust, faith, hope, belief, and confidence. When we attempt to communicate with higher beings— our angels—we are asking the higher realm to extend its energy and generosity to us. We must ask for this generosity to come to us for our highest and best and let the Universe determine what shape that will take in our lives and experiences.

Begin every angel communication with a prayer that states your intent for the highest and best, and surround yourself with light. This helps guide you to those higher beings who can assist you with your particular need or question and prepares you to receive their responses. Although you won't be going so far into the spirit realm as to enter a trance as I did in Chapter 3 where we asked for the knowledge and guidance of Elucia, you *will* want to enter a prayerful and respectful meditative state to connect to your angels. And indeed, even for experienced mediums such as myself, it all begins with a simple and elegant prayer of intent. If you can't think of your own prayer to set intent, use this one:

Infinite Spirit, God of love and light, I ask that my angels and guides come close and that I am open to receive. I ask that _____ [name your intent]. I ask that _____ [name your intent] be for the highest and the best and a healing for all concerned. I thank you so much. Amen.

Asking Questions of Your Angel Guides

The more focused the question you ask your angel—that is, the more specific your intent—the more powerful the communication will be. Although this seems only logical when you see it written here in black and white, it is easy to slip into generalities. To put the concept of proper intent in the context of the ordinary, I often tell people it's like the difference between asking, "Can you help me?" and asking, "Can you help me with the dishes tonight?"

You can even make big questions precise. You might ask, for example, "Help me find the perfect job at the perfect salary" and still get what you want. Such a question puts your trust in the Universe to know what is a perfect job and a perfect salary for you. Or you might ask, "Help me find a teaching position at a small college where the summers are hot and the winters are mild, that pays enough to let me live comfortably and enjoy some travel." This approach is specific; it refines the parameters yet leaves some room for flexibility in the response to allow the Universe to be generous.

I went to my friend Margo's house one day for lunch and she greeted me by saying, "Guess what? I'm getting married!" I got excited and gave her a big hug. "So who's the lucky man?"

"I don't know yet," she said, with the same enthusiasm that she had used to make the announcement. "I've made the decision that I'm getting married this year, and I'm putting that out there as my intent every day with my prayers."

Eight months later, Margo came to my house for lunch. "I met him," she said. "We're getting married in October." Margo had gone to a workshop shortly after our earlier lunch during which she announced her intent to get married. For one of the workshop activities, participants had to line up by birthday. She found herself standing beside Ken, who had the same birthday she did. One thing led to another, as the saying goes. Ken didn't seem daunted by Margo's desire to find a lasting love relationship; he felt encouraged! They've now been married 12 years.

Questions such as "What are the winning lottery numbers?" or "Who will be the next president of the United States?" are specific but not the kinds of questions your angels are likely to answer! Angels and spirit guides enjoy humor just as we do here on the earth plane. When you ask these kinds of questions, you might receive responses full of wit along with some food for thought.

Think about and then write down the questions you want to ask your angels. Begin your angel communication session with your prayer of intent. When you are centered and focused inward, ask that the response bring healing for the highest and the best, present your questions, and then envision whatever you've asked for as done.

You Are a Page in the *Book of Life*

Have you ever thought to ask your angel guides, "What is the purpose of my life?" Their answers are sometimes surprising and can help you become comfortable with who you *are*, rather than feeling uncomfortable about who you think you *should be*. You're perfect the way you are. So many people feel that they're not what or who they should be or that they have to do something crucially important for their lives to have meaning. But that misses the beautiful truth: We are *all* important. Some people come into this life to be movers and shakers; some are nurturers; some are teachers; others are healers. There are different meanings for *important,* but each is valid and equal to any other.

In Chapter 5, I talked about the classic movie *It's a Wonderful Life* in which Clarence the angel takes despondent George Bailey, who feels his family and friends would have been better off had he never been born, on a tour of life as it would have been had he not been in it.

Take your journal or paper and pen and go to your sacred space or someplace where you can be undisturbed for about 20 minutes. Across the top of the page write these headings:

What I Do
Who It Affects
Why It Matters
The Biggest Surprise

Under the headings, fill in activities from your daily life. Ask your angels to come and help you. Write what comes to your mind, and keep writing for 15 minutes. Then look at your lists.

What if your page in the *Book of Life* did not exist? Like George, have you discovered that even the simplest of your actions can help those around you? Simply doing the dishes for another family member, paying the toll for the car behind you on the turnpike, or giving directions to someone who is lost is an act of love and generosity, full of angel grace! The true angelic effect of your actions might indeed be your *biggest surprise!*

Receiving Responses from Your Angel Guides

In the higher realm, communication takes place through the direct exchange of energy that does not require the devices—voice, hearing, language—we humans must use here on the earth plane. An angel or higher being will connect with you and convey messages to you using your senses and capabilities. Much of my communication with angels and higher beings comes in the form of visual images, often so intense that it is difficult for me to find words to describe what I see. It is much easier when you are receiving these messages for yourself, because you can bypass the need for verbal expression and just let your mind absorb and interpret what comes to you. You move at the speed of thought, which is much faster than spoken conversation.

People receive messages from the higher realm in many ways—direct, indirect, immediate, delayed. Direct responses tend to come in forms we recognize as communication, for example thoughts, sounds, smells, and visual images. Indirect responses may be more subtle or result in outcomes that take place some distance—in either space or time—from the communication. Bob Olson's watch crystal breaking is a good example of an indirect, although immediate, response.

There are times when you ask for something and you get it, but what you receive isn't *quite* what you had in mind. Maybe you ask for the time to finish your college education and then get laid off at work. Now you have all the time you need, but can you afford to go back to school? Sometimes a situation seems ideal and then ends, such as a relationship or a job. We're devastated when it all falls apart, but as time passes, we come to realize—however slowly or quickly, joyfully or with difficulty—that we must embrace the new direction the change has set our course. And sometimes, as Father Rizzo was so fond of saying, you get the answer to your prayer and that answer is "No." What we want, what we ask for, is not always for our highest and best. But what we receive *is*.

To say yes, you have to sweat and roll up your sleeves and plunge both hands into life up to the elbows.
—Jean Anouilh (1910–1987), French playwright

So what if it seems as if you're setting your intent and asking your questions with care but you're not getting any responses from your angels? Or if you *are* getting answers, the message is flying right over your head! You might be too intently focused on your question, so much so that nothing seems to happen. You don't hear anything, see anything, or even sense anything.

Something is happening even if it is not apparent to you. Remember the Kabbalah's premise that every idea forms a ball of energy that becomes an angel (from Chapter 1)? Just the process of putting your questions, thoughts, and ideas out there creates energy ripples. And however apparently insignificant, these ripples nonetheless change the flow of energy—and your angels *always* respond when asked.

You might not experience the effects of such change for quite some time, or you might not immediately identify what happens as being a consequence of your communication with the your angels and guides in the higher realm. But pay attention to what occurs in your life after you've attempted to communicate with the Divine. What kinds of events take place in the course of your day that seem to support the help you asked your angels and guides to provide? What people come into your life unexpectedly, or what familiar people come forth with unexpected offers and assistance?

And if what you receive seems more like a trial and tribulation than a gift, begin to meditate on why a struggle is necessary and what lesson you might need to learn to grow toward your ultimate well-being and happiness. Remember, the higher realm works through whatever mechanisms here on the earth plane will be *most successful* in conveying the message or delivering the assistance and guidance you have requested. Those times when life seems its most messy and chaotic are sometimes when the angels are speaking the loudest and helping us the most! Each day is a privilege to learn, to grow, to try again. That is why we are human, that is why we are *here*. From their vantage point in the higher realm, our angel guides are uniquely positioned—*they* learn from our humanity, as they assist us from Spirit on *our* earthly journey of learning.

Bringing Closure to Your Angel Communication Session

Just as you opened your angel session with intent, you need to close the session with intent. As you learned in Chapter 3 when we called upon Elucia, during communication with the higher realm your chakras are open to receive the Divine energy and messages that come to you. Leaving the chakras open after the angel session drains too much energy and positions you for possible exposure to receiving all kinds of energy that will quickly overwhelm you. So at the end of the session you must return to the mundane. This is like turning on and off a light switch. The energy remains available; all you do is restrict its access.

You may close your angel session in a variety of ways, but it is important that you always bring the session to an *official close*. Visualize your upper chakras (crown, brow or third eye, throat, and heart) closing like the petals of a flower might close at sunset. Or visualize each chakra color fading from bright to dark. You can pass your hand over your upper chakras as you do this visualization. See each chakra closing like a door—but remember *close*, never lock, the door. Or visualize surrounding yourself with white light or a white bubble—Divine protection to reestablish your personal energy boundaries. You have allowed your energy to be open and accessible during communication with the higher realm; now you want to protect that access.

Bringing closure also should always include a thank you to the Divine. I say a short prayer of thanks similar to this:

Infinite Spirit, God of Love and Light, I give thanks for all you have shared. I give thanks to my spirit guides and angels for their guidance and assistance with _____
[name your intent]. I go in love. I go in peace. I go in gratitude. Amen.

Reflect on the communication and the information imparted to you by your angels and spirit guides, then record the session by writing about it in your journal. Include not only what was said, felt, seen, heard, even smelled, but also what impressions and conditions surrounded the session and how these influenced and informed the communication.

Activating Your Physical and Spiritual Senses

When you communicate, whether with the co-worker at the desk across from yours or a being from the higher realm, you do so through an integration of your physical and spiritual senses. Many people are most aware of the input they receive through their physical senses—vision, hearing, smell, taste, and touch. These correspond with your spiritual senses of clairvoyance (inner vision), clairaudience (inner hearing), clairsentience (inner knowing), and intuition (inner feeling). Energy, in endless forms—including your angels—stimulates all these senses to bring you messages, both mundane and Divine. Understanding how to activate your physical and spiritual senses will enhance your angel communication sessions.

Using Chakra Energy

Your chakra energy centers enable your body to connect its inner energy with the outer energy of the Universe at large. They open and close, somewhat like valves, to regulate the level of connection. Mostly they do this without your conscious awareness; your higher self guides your openness. Learning to direct this regulation with conscious intent gives you the ability to expand your experience of the Divine. Of the seven major chakras, four of them—throat, heart, brow or third eye, and crown—are especially important for communicating with the higher realm. The energy vibrations that stimulate your five physical senses also stimulate and open the chakras. These are some of the ways the energy of your physical and intuitive senses integrate.

The Chakras of Higher Realm Communication

	Heart (Fourth) Chakra	Throat (Fifth) Chakra	Brow or Third Eye (Sixth) Chakra	Crown (Seventh) Chakra
Energy	Emotions and feelings	Truth and voice	Inner vision and intuition	Divine Spirit
Colors	Green, pink	Bright blue, turquoise	Deep blue-violet, indigo	Violet, opalescent white
Fragrances and essences	Rose, jasmine, marjoram, yarrow	Chamomile, lemongrass, sage, sandalwood	Eucalyptus, lavender, peppermint, rosemary	Boswellia, frankincense, lavender, myrrh
Chants and sacred sounds	*Yam*	*Ham*	*Ah*	*Om*
Yoga postures	Camel	Fish	Seated mudra	Seated mudra, headstand, hare
Crystals and minerals	Emerald, rose quartz, tourmaline	Agate, azurite, onyx, tiger's eye, turquoise	Lapis lazuli, fluorite	Amethyst, diamond

Energy and Color: Light and Flame

Fire is the most primal source of energy in our physical world. Even before humankind harnessed flame, we knew that the sun was the source of heat, light, and life itself. The flame of a candle draws the focus of the mind and emotions. It helps us feel movement and stillness at once. We can allow our energies, especially the energies of stress and negativity, to release into the atmosphere as the flame does. We also can experience the merging of Divine energy with our personal energy, much as oxygen from the atmosphere merges with the burning candle to sustain the flame. We can add color and fragrance to candles to expand our sensory (physical and spiritual) experience of them, opening wide our chakras to invite our spirit guides and angels to merge with us. The vibration of the flame's yellow-orange color supports and enhances grounded wisdom, creativity, and openness. Yellow, orange, and red are the colors of the lower chakras, the chakras that ground us to the earth, our sensual emotions, and our willpower.

Looking at the flame atop a candle that is the color of one of the four higher chakras or envisioning those colors during candle meditation allows us to experience the energy of their vibrations grounded by the flame's intensity. These higher vibrations can assist us in connecting to our angels and guides on an intuitive level.

- **Green and pink are colors of balance, calm, and health.** Focus on these colors when asking questions about health or relationship.

- **Blue is the color of the quest.** When you are seeking answers of Spirit, focus on various shades of blue. The more intense the shade of blue, the greater the depth of information and enlightenment that will come to you.

- **Purple, or violet, and white are the colors of Spirit.** Focus on purple to intensify your connection with the energy of the Divine. Envision white for protection and sanctuary so you may feel safe in opening yourself so fully.

- **Turquoise and other variations of blue-green are calming and soothing.** Surround yourself with these colors when meditating to relieve stress, worry, and anxiety, and to release your fears.

Fragrances and Essences

Fragrances directly stimulate our sense of smell as well as send vibrational waves of energy through our chakras. We can experience this energy through herbs, essential oils, and incense (plus, the smoke from burning incense intensifies the energy experience).

Even when we don't actually smell fragrances, as with flower essences, their energies affect us intuitively. Herbs, fragrances, and essences support opening our personal energy to connect with the energy of the Divine in different ways depending on the character of the substance's energy. Chamomile, lavender, and peppermint are soothing and calming, for example. Boswellia, frankincense, and myrrh vibrate at high frequencies that stimulate the spiritual senses of clairvoyance, clairaudience, clairsentience, and intuition. Eucalyptus and rose are healing. Rosemary, sage, sandalwood, and thyme heighten the mind's focus. You might find that you enjoy using fragrances and essences during your angel communication sessions.

Chants and Sacred Sounds

Sounds and music are energy vibrations that occur at frequencies the ear can detect. Each of the chakras is sensitive to a particular frequency. You can activate a chakra through chanting a sound at its specific frequency. Although the pitch of the sound might not be in your personal key, it nonetheless has the effect of the frequency when you chant. People chanting together in groups naturally create beautiful harmonies that focus the frequency much like a magnifying glass can focus the rays of the sun so intensely as to start a fire.

To chant, start off with three deep cleansing breaths. Then take another deep breath in from your diaphragm. As you exhale, again from the diaphragm, let the sound come out for the duration of the exhaled breath. These sounds activate the various higher chakras, and you can feel this happen. As you become more adept at chanting, you'll find that you can hold the sound longer. Always chant in the order of the chakras. To open communication with the higher realm, you'll want to focus on opening the four upper chakras. The chants are as follows:

- Heart (fourth) chakra: *Yam*
- Throat (fifth) chakra: *Ham*
- Brow or third eye (sixth) chakra: *Ah*
- Crown (seventh) chakra: *Om*

Music also opens and activates the chakras, which is one reason so many spiritual and religious ceremonies incorporate singing and song. Singing brings in the sounds of the chant, and the song, or music, adds depth and intensity through the resonation of the notes. Try playing different kinds of music during your angel communication sessions, and observe how they affect the experience.

In the Light: A Song of Chant

Put these chants together in patterns of sound to compose a more extended chant that is like an esoteric song. Then sit in lotus pose, half-lotus pose, or cross-legged with your back straight and chant your song. Feel the resonation of each tone in your body as the tone activates the corresponding chakra. Think of one of your favorite songs, a song you like to listen to because it makes you feel happy or peaceful or just good. Can you sing or hum that song in ways that create these same resonances within your body? Can you hear your angels singing with you?

Joining Body, Mind, and Spirit: Yoga

Yoga is an exercise of the mind, body, and spirit. When you bring your mind and the body into alignment, the spirit embodies the union. This establishes a harmony within your being. You can't really separate the three components of mind, body, and spirit: They are one. In the concentration of holding a pose, you can actually feel your essential energy and its connection to the Divine.

Yoga postures are about balance. When you create balance of mind and body, you allow the spirit to soar. Tree pose is a basic yoga posture that emphasizes balance and grounds you to the earth as you reach toward the heavens. To do tree pose ...

1. Start in mountain pose. Stand with your feet flat on the floor, your big toes touching. Your back and head should be erect. As you reach up through your crown chakra at the top of your head, extend your hands, palms facing your body, down toward the earth. Feel your shoulders lower. Breathe and relax your hands. You are a mountain spirit.

2. Now, bring your hands up and place them in namaste, or prayer— your palms flat together with your fingertips pointed upward. Rest your thumbs in front of your heart chakra.

3. Lift your right foot and place it against the inside of your left leg, opening your hip to turn your knee outward. Place your foot as high against your leg as you can while holding your body in balance and alignment—that could be your inner thigh, your calf, or the inside of your ankle with your toes touching the floor. Breathe and center your spirit.

4. When you are ready, raise your hands over your head, keeping your palms together if you can do so and keep your balance or separating your hands to remain stable. Breathe slowly and evenly. Feel the Divine reach down to take your hands.

5. Feel the energy of this Divine connection flow into your being.

6. Reverse your movements until you are again in mountain pose, then repeat with the other foot raised to balance the pose's benefit.

7. Finally, once again in mountain pose, close your eyes and allow your mind to visualize what it needs to incorporate the Divine energy of this pose into your being. Envision it as so.

The Crystal Channel

In Chapter 2, we created an angel window by hanging small faceted crystals in a window where they could refract the incoming light. Crystals are well known for their ability to receive and transmit energy. Before the age of modern electronics, radios used crystals to pluck signals of certain frequencies from the air that the radio's transformer tubes then converted to recognizable sounds such as words and music. Every ham radio operator knew that the bigger and clearer the crystal, the stronger the reception range. Although most radio equipment today uses electronic receptors rather than crystals, crystals remain powerful tools for channeling energy. And you can use crystals to facilitate your connections with the energy of the Divine.

First you need to get a crystal. Shops that sell metaphysical items carry crystals, as do some craft and hobby stores. You want a quartz crystal to use during crystal channeling. Look for Atlantian crystals or Lemurian seed crystals, as they hold the energy (and its wisdom) of these ancient and lost civilizations—although you can use a regular clear crystal just as well. Some people prefer polished crystals; other people choose rough crystals. Some people like crystals with lots of inclusions; others opt for complete clarity. Choose a crystal that appeals to *you*. You should like the way it looks and feels.

To use your crystal to create a channel of communication between your higher self and the higher realm of your angels and guides ...

1. Go to your sacred place or a quiet place where you can be undisturbed. Establish your intent for the highest and best, and ask your spirit guides and angels to be with you.

2. Hold the crystal between your hands. If there is a natural surface that your thumbs or fingers want to rub, rub it. Otherwise, gently rub the crystal's largest facet.

3. Ask a question, if you have one, or just allow yourself to receive the energy that comes through the crystal. The crystal might become warm or cool as the energy changes.

4. When you are finished, close your chakras and say a prayer of gratitude. Hold the crystal in your open hands for a few moments to allow its energy to clear.

Tools of Divine Communication

In our everyday communications with people in our lives, we use various tools—voice and speech, eyes and sight, ears and hearing—to express and receive messages. When extending the communication process to the broader energy of the Universe at large, we need to expand our methods to accommodate the intensified nature of the process.

Are you familiar with bandwidth and electronic communication, such as with Internet connections, cordless telephones, and cellular telephones? The speed with which electronic signals can travel via conventional "land line" connections is restricted by the physical capacity of the connection—wires. Sophisticated wireless devices—broadband connections—dispel this limitation to allow more signals to stream through in the same amount of time. Your physical senses are like land lines; your spiritual senses are like broadband connections.

Angels come down and put ideas into people's heads and then people are very proud because they think they're their ideas.
—Dudley the Angel (played by Cary Grant) in *The Bishop's Wife* (1947)

Intuition

Intuition means "inner feeling," such as when you know who is calling when the phone rings. Inspiration is when ideas just come to you and those ideas lead to a creative act. On a mundane level, it's like being at a party or an event and you say something absolutely brilliant—so brilliant that it surprises even you—and you say to yourself, *Where did that come from?*

Where *does* that come from? I call it a form of Divine inspiration. Your angels and spirit guides are watching out for you, and when they see that you need a little help, they send it to you. Then it comes from you as if it were your original thought. Could it be? Who knows!

For some people, intuition just happens. They have no outward or tangible presentations of their intuitive knowledge. Other people experience intuitive knowledge in ways that activate their physical experiences. This is how intuition works for Bob Olson, who feels a tingling sensation in his body when his intuition is activated. As he follows the direction in which his intuition leads him, the tingling intensifies. One of Bob's most memorable experiences with this was when he went to his grandmother's burial at the same cemetery in which he knew his great-great-grandfather Julius was also buried. Although Julius had died before Bob was born, Bob had always felt a close connection to him, and I had done a spirit drawing of Julius for Bob.

Bob's grandmother, Julius's great-granddaughter, had told Bob that Julius was buried in that particular cemetery, but she hadn't been able to remember the location of the grave. So from his grandmother's grave, Bob took off walking. Although there were thousands and thousands of graves in this cemetery, Bob walked in a direct path for about a quarter of a mile. When he stopped, he felt certain Julius's grave would be there ... but it wasn't. Disappointed, Bob stood waiting for his wife to catch up with him. "It's not here," Bob told her. "Yes, it is," she said, and she pointed to a gravestone just ahead of where they were standing. Bob walked over and, sure enough, it was Julius's grave. Finding Julius's physical resting place became another tangible element in Bob's connection to his great-great-grandfather. The angels, through Bob's intuition, had led him there.

Meditation

Meditation is a process of focusing on a particular thought or image so that it becomes, with your breath, the center of your awareness. This frees your conscious mind from the busy-ness of the thoughts that ordinarily clutter it to join with your higher self.

If you are new to meditation, you might find it easier to follow a guided meditation. Many of the exercises at the end of the chapters in this book can be done as guided meditations; you can have someone read them to you, or you can read them yourself into a tape recorder and then play back the tape. Fragrances, candles, colors, sounds (chanting or music), and yoga help you prepare your mind for meditation just as they help you open your chakras.

Visualization: Seeing It as So

I often tell people, "Visualize what you want and then visualize it as so. Once you can see something, it becomes tangible to you." This isn't always as easy as it sounds; our mental roadblocks go up pretty quickly when we are opening ourselves to the potential of change. Visualization is a good way to end a meditation or communication with the higher side. If visualizing what you want is difficult, ask your spirit guides and angels to help you ... and to help you maintain the visualization after you finish your meditation or communication so you can make it manifest in your life.

Light Works: Focusing Intent

The mandala is a useful tool for focusing intent and guiding meditation. You can make your own mandala to use for this meditation exercise (I tell you how to make a mandala in Chapter 5). You also need your journal or a piece of paper and a pen.

1. Write a specific question at the top of your paper.
2. Take three deep, cleansing breaths in through your nose and out through your mouth.
3. Ask your spirit guides and angels to come in.
4. Look into your mandala and follow its patterns into its center or focal point. Concentrate on the focal point, and set your mind free.
5. Stay in this meditative state until it feels complete to you. You might not feel the response immediately.
6. Read your question again, then immediately begin writing to allow your mind to free-associate the answer. Write until you feel you are finished.

While You Were Sleeping ...

Our spirit guides and angels often come to us through dreams. We expect dreams to be surrealistic and are open to the messages they convey to us through their vivid imagery.

Frank had a series of dreams in which he saw his friend Paula pregnant—big pregnant, with an enormous belly. In these dreams, Frank could see into Paula's belly, and he could see three babies snuggled together. The first few times Frank had this dream he told Paula about it, who laughed. "How silly," she said. "I'm not pregnant. I don't even have a man in my life right now." About six months later, Paula did have a man in her life, and one afternoon she called Frank. She told him that she was pregnant. And guess what? She was carrying triplets!

Sometimes dreams can provide a forum for intentional communication with the higher realm, letting your higher self question and interact with your spirit guides and angels without being blocked by your rational mind. You can encourage such communication by setting the intent as you are falling asleep. As when you are initiating contact with the higher realm when you are awake, establish your intent for the highest and best and surround yourself with the protection of white light. When you wake up in the morning, say a brief prayer of thanks, write everything you can remember about your dreams, then free-associate any additional information that comes to you.

Don't worry whether what you're putting down makes any sense; just get it down before, as tends to happen with dreams, your conscious mind overwrites it with all the thoughts that fill it when you are awake. Later, you can pull out your notes and read through them. What thoughts and images do the words trigger? Meditate on or journal about those that strike you. Revisit this dream communication every few weeks or months. You might be surprised by the connections that continue to emerge.

Highest and Best: Opening Your Third Eye Chakra

Most of us on a spiritual path crave to have inner sight or clairvoyance. We crave to be in touch with the intuition that helps us perceive the higher realm. The third eye chakra is located in the center of your brow about an inch above your eyebrows. Not surprisingly, when the third eye is blocked, you might experience headaches, nightmares, or difficulty with vision. Visualization, colors, fragrances, and chanting can help open your third eye chakra. Visualize the color indigo or deep blue-violet, and draw from the energy of crystals such as lapis lazuli or florite. Rosemary, lavender, or peppermint help open the third eye chakra as well, as does chanting the sound "Ah."

Sit in a meditative pose such as lotus. Take a deep breath pulled in from your diaphragm. As you allow your diaphragm to slowly push out the breath, allow your vocal cords to form the sound "Ah." Let the sound extend for the full length of the exhalation. Continue to chant until you feel the cloudiness lift from your mind. Some people can see sounds, tastes, and smells when their third eye chakra is open.

The seated mudra yoga posture also can facilitate the opening of the third eye. As you sit in this pose, visualize your angel or guide seated in the same pose across from you. Breathe as they breathe, as you breathe together. Here's how to enter the pose:

1. Begin by sitting cross-legged on the floor, your left foot balanced on your right knee and your right foot balanced on your left knee. Or if you are flexible enough, from a cross-legged position, take your left foot in your right hand and draw your leg across until your knees are stacked one above the other in front of you. Your feet will rest on either side by your hips. Hold your big toes.

2. Take three deep, cleansing breaths, breathing in through your nose and out through your mouth. Take the first breath in to clear your

body, then slowly release the breath. Take the second breath to open your mind, and take a third breath to free your spirit.

3. Lace your fingers behind you at the sacrum (near your tailbone), and stretch your hands downward. Open your chest and lower your shoulders by moving your shoulder blades back. If this motion is too difficult for you, extend both arms over your head, fingertips reaching upward as you again keep your shoulders lowered and even.

4. In either position from step 3, bend forward at the hips until you can't go any farther.

5. Bring your forehead (third eye) to rest on your knee, your leg, or the floor, if you can.

6. Relax and breathe in the energy of this posture.

7. When you are ready, release the posture and return to a seated meditative pose. Close your eyes and allow your mind to visualize what it needs to incorporate the energy of this pose into your being. Envision it as so. Thank your angel guide for sharing the pose with you and lending Divine energy to your effort.

Always remember this: Whether you are doing an "official" angel communication session or just doing *anything,* your angels are with you, communicating, guiding, and ready for your questions.

Chapter 9

Angel Messages

You've opened the lines of communication with your angels with clear intent. In every angel session, you are working with the tools of heightened perception and intuition so you can strengthen the energetic flow of Divine inspiration through your human body. You feel this energy pulse and breathe awareness into the instruments of your senses, sharpening your ability to see and helping you reach ever higher to hear heavenly voices and touch your angels.

Sometimes, after a focused angel session, you might come back to Earth grounded and centered with the bliss of having spent some quality time harmonizing with the Eternal. The message of the session might be as simple—and as profound— as this: *You are loved. You are one with all that is. You are one with the angels in the presence of the Divine.* Allowing this energy to enter our being and accepting its universal truth is accepting the Light within ourselves and within each being of Spirit. Understanding this message is the essence of what it means to be enlightened, empowered, immortal, and alive. However, "coming down" from the heavens means you do indeed have to "hit the ground," and the experience of coming back into your earthly day-to-day existence might seem jarring or even a little bit unfair. (It is nice up there in the ethereal realm!) Remember the feelings and emotions I described in Chapter 3 after traveling through an advanced trance state to contact the angelic being Elucia to receive her angel messages for you. Going up is easy; returning to our bodies and earthly lives can be quite a shock to the system.

Once you have glimpsed the eternal in what you receive through a focused angel communication, the goal to strive for in living every day is to remember that this angelic light is available to you with every breath and with every moment of your being. It is available even when it might not feel that way, when you cannot perceive the light that guides you, or when you are unable to reach the same height of bliss and peace every time you try to connect and converse with your angels. The truth is something you already know, or have certainly arrived at by now, this far into *Empowering Your Life with Angels:* Angelic messages are all around you, all the time. Whether you become consciously aware of these messages in angel sessions or are unconsciously receiving them as you go about your daily life, your angels and guides speak to you every moment of every day.

Music of the Spheres

What could your angels possibly be telling you in the singular tones singing out the message of Divine wholeness, the peace that passes understanding, the open lotus blossom of enlightenment, the Music of the Spheres? You think you hear *something,* but what? How can you know that the messages you've received are really from an angel and not simply an airy figment of your imagination or the tranquil high of meditation? In this chapter, I want to give you insights about how you can identify, understand, and interpret the opportunities and challenges presented among the myriad individual angel messages you receive, intended and directed by the Divine uniquely and especially for your highest and best. I'll help you work with messages from your angels that are mundane and practical, designed to help you weather life's vicissitudes. I also want to give you some advanced harmonic tools for maintaining, nurturing, and encouraging your personal connection with the angelic Light so you can learn how to hold this connection and carry it with you.

Celestial Harmony: Connecting the Earth and Angelic Realms

We discovered in Chapter 8 that certain forms of music such as chants and hymns call the angels to come to us and relate to opening specific chakra energy centers that help us receive angel messages from Spirit. Celestial music has ancient origins, dating to the sixth century B.C.E. It was the father of mathematics himself, Pythagoras, who discovered the Music of the Spheres.

Playing around with some string one day, Pythagoras discovered that interrupting a plucked string's vibration at the string's halfway point produced the same note as when plucking the string's full length, because the half-length note vibrated at twice the frequency of the full-length note. The distance between these sounds was that of eight notes—an octave. Each point along the string that could then be halved and at which a secondary note could be produced marked an interval. The convergence of sound between the primary and secondary notes became known as a harmonic. The longer the string, in theory, the more harmonic possibilities exist. The most intriguing array of these possibilities float on the harp, with its many long strings establishing innumerable harmonics called overtones.

In Pythagoras's time, the prevailing perception of the design of the Universe held that the planets were spheres occupying fixed positions in the heavens, in a linear path from the earth to heaven. These positions aligned like the intervals in an octave. Music, ancient philosophers believed, embodied the energy of the Universe, and each planet had a unique vibratory frequency. Because the planets aligned at intervals, the vibration of one produced a sound as well as activated sounds among its harmonics. This idea became known as the Music of the Spheres.

The harp's overtones became associated with the Music of the Spheres, and many ancient philosophers posited the premise that this music marked the path of communication between the gods and humans. Certain aspects of this premise melded into monotheistic belief systems of later centuries, giving rise to the belief that the harp is the instrument of angels and that we can summon the angels through harp music. Other instruments with long, multiple strings such as the sitar and the modern guitar can produce harmonics limited to perhaps three or four overtones, depending on the primary note and the musician's skill to "split" the string with just the right placement and weight of touch.

Musicologists point out that the music of The Beatles, with its range of instrumentation—including the sitar—contains overtones, harmonics, and rhythms extraordinarily similar, translated into the language of mathematics that is the foundation of all music, to the Music of the Spheres. Could it be that the Fab Four were communing with the angelic realms when they recorded their landmark *White* album?

In the rich abundance of angel imagery from the late Middle Ages and the Renaissance, we often see angels playing harps, lyres, and lutes. The belief evolved that making the same sounds as these heavenly instruments allowed us humans to bridge the language barrier and communicate directly with the angels. This belief held that upon hearing us send to the heavens the notes they themselves used to beckon each other, the angels would come down to Earth to see what we wanted. (Steven Spielberg used this kind of communication as a guiding metaphor to portray humanity's first "official" contact with extraterrestrial beings in his classic film *Close Encounters of the Third Kind*.) Music came to permeate all kinds of spiritual and religious celebrations, from weddings to funerals to gatherings of worship across denominational and cultural boundaries.

Rita's drawing, Meditation, *captures the power and intensity of the monk's connection to the Divine. Although the symbol here is a cross, a profound relationship to the Divine goes beyond any one religious doctrine. Christian, Muslim, Jew, Buddhist, Pagan, Wiccan—we are all connected to the Source.*

Across time and continents, Gregorian monks in Western Europe and Tibetan monks in Eastern Asia chanted the same tones to commune with the angels. The chant is deceptive in its simplicity. Nearly everyone—this includes you, too!—can make the single-note, single-syllable sounds of the basic chants. Maybe this is so because the energy of the sound resonates to the body's energy patterns, maybe because the notes are easy for the vocal cords to form, or maybe because the sounds happen to be strikingly similar to the first noncrying sounds humans make. Whatever the reason, chant leaders are able to hold groups of dozens to hundreds of voices together on the same note, at the same pitch, for extended chanting sessions to produce flows of sound that certainly must be as pleasing to celestial ears as to human ears.

In Chapter 8, I introduced a beginning exercise to chant the ancient sounds associated with the heart, throat, third eye, and crown chakras. As you know, the crown chakra, our energy connection to the Universe and the Divine, resonates to the *Om* tone. Even the prayer-closing *amen* familiar in Judaic and Christian practices is said to be a variation of the *Om* chant, derived from the Eastern phonetic spelling of the syllable as *Aum*. *Amen* actually opens the crown chakra, clearing the way for your prayer message to leave you for the Divine. When you ask the angels to carry your messages upward, end your request with *Om* or *amen* to facilitate this energy transfer. Then, to remember your grounding on Earth, gently close your crown chakra by envisioning the open petals of a lotus blossom slowly folding in upon themselves.

Light Works: Celestial Tones

In this exercise, you will use an advanced chakra chant and a pitch pipe to identify the specific notes that call to the angels through the Music of the Spheres. At your local music store, you'll find different pitch pipes for various instruments and purposes; look for one that has any or all of the notes B, A, F#, and G# (that's F-sharp and G-sharp if you don't remember your musicology). These notes correspond with the chant syllables as follows:

B   *Om* (or *Aum*, in its Eastern representation), the note of the crown chakra

A   *Ah*, the note of the third eye chakra

F#   *Ham*, the note of the throat chakra

G#   *Yam*, the note of the heart chakra

143

Sound one of these notes on your pitch pipe. Experiment with it, making it long, short, soft, and loud. Become familiar just with the sound until you can hear it in your head without the pitch pipe. Hear it? Good!

Now, breathe in and breathe out three slow, deep breaths, in through your nose and out through your mouth. Breathe in one ... two ... three ... four ... five; breathe out one ... two ... three ... four ... five. Feel your breath enter your throat, travel to your lungs, fill your lungs, and move to every cell in your body. Notice the rhythm of your breathing and how it calms your body and your mind. Notice, too, the path of the breath retreating from your body and returning to the atmosphere.

Put the pitch pipe to your lips, and take a breath in over the count of five. When you breathe out, blow through the pitch pipe in the same pattern, one ... two ... three ... four ... five. Listen to the sound. Breathe in and breathe out through the pitch pipe over the count of five. Again, listen to the sound.

Keep doing this until the sound you make is steady and consistent, whether you are breathing in or breathing out. This takes a bit of concentration. Take a break if you get tired. If you feel lightheaded, you're breathing too fast—slow down!

Next, breathe in through the pitch pipe over the count of five, remove the pitch pipe from your lips, and when you breathe out, let the same sound as the note on the pitch pipe come through your own vocal cords. Form the sound for the count of five. Use the earlier chant syllable for the note you are playing.

As you chant the note for Om, *the crown chakra, hold the image of the Sanskrit symbol for the sound in your mind and heart.*

Practice this pattern—in through the pitch pipe, out through your vocal cords—until the sounds match. Practice each note, one at a time until, it sounds clear and true.

Now, hear and feel the sounds for each of the notes as they enter your ear and resonate throughout your body, then leave and return to the energy of the Universe. Can you feel the sound follow the path of your breathing, your life force, carrying vital energy to all the cells in your body? Practice with the notes until they are familiar. We'll be coming back to them later in this chapter.

As you learn to resonate your life force in tune with the celestial Music of the Spheres, you will find that your energy is open to receive angel messages, even as you perfect your harmonic call to angel ears. With this eternal connection between your earthly physical vessel and the angelic realm of Light and Spirit strong and intact, you are empowered to exchange information, act, grow, discover, and do all that is possible. You become open to receive.

Open to Receive

Sometimes listening to and heeding our angel messages means we have to be willing to do what seems unconventional; that we need to take something, or someone, on faith; or that we need to listen and believe. In the scheme of it all, in the light of the Universe, our own small efforts have a way of joining a whole that is so much bigger than we can envision or imagine. What angel voice is calling you right now, and how are you responding?

Go the Distance

"If you build it, he will come," whispers an ethereal voice in the 1989 movie *Field of Dreams*. Unsure even himself whether he's going crazy or whether he's on the verge of the miraculous, struggling farmer and lifelong baseball aficionado Ray Kinsella (played by Kevin Costner) heeds the message, plows under a field of corn, and converts it into a regulation ball field complete with lights and stands for the fans. When baseball legend Shoeless Joe Jackson walks onto the diamond, Ray thinks maybe he has understood the message—the field is for Shoeless Joe's spiritual redemption. As every baseball fan knows, Shoeless Joe was banned from baseball in 1921, despite his acquittal from a jury trial, in the wake of accusations that he and seven teammates conspired

to throw the 1919 World Series. But the messages continue, and with every plot twist in *Field of Dreams* it becomes apparent that Ray must continue to work to understand what he is supposed to do and learn. It isn't as simple or as easy as just Shoeless Joe.

"*Ease his pain,*" the soft voice insists. "*Go the distance.*" If you've seen the movie, you know that all the characters in it, whether portraying baseball spirits or human beings on the earth plane, are blessed and healed as they each grapple to understand the angelic message in their individual presences on Ray's field of dreams. This is especially true for Ray who discovers he has done more than facilitate the compassionate building of a field where others can come for Divine inspiration, forgiveness, transformation, and fun! Ray discovers that the field is the place of his own healing, once he opens himself to receive. Before a cathartic catch with his father John, a former major league catcher who returns from Spirit to play on the field of dreams, John asks Ray if the field is heaven. "No," Ray answers. "It's Iowa." At last, in a moment of epiphany and grace, Ray understands that his father has not come so Ray can heal John's pain over their estranged relationship in life. Rather, John has come to heal and restore *Ray*.

> And is there enough magic out there in the moonlight to make this dream come true?
> —Burt Lancaster, as Doc "Moonlight" Graham in *Field of Dreams*

We sometimes might be slow to recognize our angels and catch their messages, but both are there for us in our lives, every day. Heaven is Iowa; Iowa is heaven. All we need to do is look, listen, and be open to receive. Go ahead, go the distance, and step up to the plate. What would be your *personal* field of dreams? Is there an ethereal voice whispering—or shouting—for your attention?

In the Light: Trust the Message

Often we don't understand when callings are coming to us. Most of the time messages come to us through the mundane world around us. The everyday world is our field of dreams, the magical diamond of angel messages, the proving ground for celestial harmonies. Divine messages come through the mundane images and objects that relentlessly pull our attention in certain, sometimes unexpected, directions. While we're listening for voices from above, the angels send real messages that are coming in from all around us, honing us toward a particular frequency for understanding. Even in connection with the Divine, we must always remember to keep our feet firmly planted on the ground. Look around you, here on the earth plane. Are you paying attention? Are you tuning in to the angel messages manifesting for *you*, right now?

For a few weeks or even an entire month, carry around a notepad and pen to keep track of the words, colors, images, and emotions that consistently appear with synchronicity in your daily life or in your dreams. Also write down the context surrounding each such appearance—did you see the image on a billboard, hear the song on the radio, or find the article on the Internet? Are you offered the same taste or drawn to a particular color? What patterns emerge in the events, impressions, and activities of each day? Do the messages of these patterns make sense to you when you look at them in layer upon layer of experience? Do they surprise you? Do you immediately connect to something profound hidden there? Or do you suddenly see the answer to a question that is vexing you, something as simple as what color to paint your home office to something more nuanced as recognizing generosity in your life or learning how to see a friend or partner in a new light. Write a few words to describe each pattern you detect in your experience and the angelic message you believe the pattern might represent.

The Face of an Angel

When we find ourselves in a moment of need, our angel message comes through loud and clear. There's no need to wait for layers or patterns to nudge us to a new direction or new realization. And if it is necessary, the angel will bring the message directly to us and intercede on our behalf. When was the last time *you* saw the face of an angel?

A pharmaceutical representative with a broad territory to cover, Christine logged more hours behind the wheel than many long-haul truckers. She confidently drove in all kinds of weather, could change a tire in 15 minutes, and checked her oil every Tuesday. But on a recent Thursday, she overlooked one *tiny* detail. She was orienting a new rep, they had a lot of pavement to cover, and their next destination was a presentation for a convention of cardiologists. Suddenly Christine's Camry shimmied, shuddered, and stopped. Christine looked at the gauges on the dashboard—*empty,* read the one that measured the car's gasoline level.

Thankfully, Christine was able to coast safely to the shoulder near an off-ramp. She could see a service station on the road just at the end of the ramp. The two women got out of the car and started pushing it along the shoulder. All was rolling right along until the off-ramp took an incline. A pick-up truck pulled in behind them and the driver leaned out the window. "Need a push?" he asked.

Christine eased her car to a stop in front of the gasoline pump, said a brief prayer of gratitude, and got out to thank the generous Good Samaritan. But in short time, he was gone! Christine filled the car's gas tank, and the two women were soon back on the road. "Too bad he didn't stick around," said the rep in training. "He was one good-looking young man!"

"What?" Christine turned to the other woman in surprise. "It was kind of him to give us a push, but he looked older than my grandfather!" Their roadside savior, the two women discovered, appeared to each of them as each might perceive someone who was safe and could be trusted. Our angelic helpers bring us the assistance we need in the forms we will trust and accept.

It is in rugged crises, in unweariable endurance, and in aims which put sympathy out of the question, that the angel is shown.
—Ralph Waldo Emerson (1803–1882), American philosopher and writer

You Get What You Need for *Now*

Sometimes the messages we receive seem truly heaven-sent yet turn out to have entirely different meanings than we originally thought.

Mark was going through a difficult time in his life. Not much seemed to be going right for him, and he felt really down about his love life in particular. Every time he met a woman he thought he could become serious about, something happened to separate them. Last summer she was Julie, who got accepted into graduate school—across the country. Then was Carmen, who got the promotion she wanted—along with a transfer to the company's office in Nova Scotia. And now Rebecca, whose National Guard unit was being activated for duty, was going to leave. Confused, all Mark knew was that he yearned for someone to share his life with. Yet all he received in answer to his prayers for a life partner, it seemed, were lovely ladies with whom he was destined to have only short-term, geographically undesirable relationships.

We tend to view life as a sequence of end results rather than a continuous journey with twists, turns, and even switchbacks along the way. We want to jump right to the end, right to the success, the goal. If we look to our angels and spirit guides to lift and carry us effortlessly on their gossamer wings and drop us lightly and gently upon the attainment of our deepest desires, perhaps we need to cultivate a new mind-set. Perhaps if Mark learned to lift *himself* to a new place (his angels and guides in tow, of course!), he would be able to take a new view and see the possibility that long-term love and stability come from more than a fixed spot on the map.

The messages of our angels are not always easily seen or understood by us (much less acted upon!), but their guidance is with us *for the here and now*. Mark might have needed the pain and heartache of losing love— as well as the hopeful experience of having three wonderful potential partners come into his life—to understand the courage that comes with staying the course, from learning at last how to honor what we receive. Because Mark finally realized this new mind-set, he and Rebecca are planning to marry before she must report to duty.

No matter what is happening in our lives, our angels are with us to guide us, protect us, and help us *right now*. Trust that you will get what you need, and remember always the angelic light that shines in your heart.

What becomes of lost opportunities? Perhaps our guardian angel gathers them up and will give them back when we've grown older and wiser—and will use them rightly.
—Helen Keller (1880–1968), American writer

Angel Messages and Karma

People (and angels!) often enter our lives because we have karma— unfinished lessons we carry from the past—to work through. Our connections might be strong, even intense, but they don't last any longer than the Divine contracts we negotiated, on the soul level, to facilitate the necessary learning. And they are no more pleasant or painful than what we *need* so that we may learn, grow, and work toward enlightenment. We have to remember that we receive angelic messages for where we are *right now*, for what we need *right now*.

Angelic messages from Spirit come for the time and experiences of the present because that's what we can handle. Most of us can't handle what waits for us 10 steps—or 10 years—down the road. What we *can* handle is information that relates to the *here and now*. The circumstances surrounding our experiences and relationships might feel as if they are unchangeable, beyond our control, or that what is happening now will *always* be happening. But it is only here on the earth plane that time and space and distance exist. For the angels, all time is *now;* all place is *everywhere.*

When we encounter obstacles, difficult people, even devils in angel clothes, or when it seems that we're surrounded by "bad karma," we must look closely and understand that *all* experiences contain an enduring, timeless angelic message to comfort and bless us where we stand *now.* Those who bring us signs are not always those whom we expect; bless the people and the angels who touch your life as they come and go. Live in what is *now.* Look for your messages and your answers in what is happening *now.* The potential for all time lives in each moment. We are healed in each moment. We heal others in each moment. To ground and center your spirit in this knowledge, offer this prayer to your angels and to the Source of All Knowledge:

All that I am, all that I have been, all that I will be, help me to see and understand all is now.

Holograms: Messages in the Light

Holograms, like angels, are full of light. We already know that the harp can produce the most advanced harmonics, or overtones, to approximate celestial music. The different wavelengths of light beams, producing all the colors of the rainbow, can each be considered a harp string to be plucked. Holograms are recorded images of light wave interference. An object beam and a reference beam of laser light are used to make a hologram. The reference beam is aimed directly at the holographic plate while the object beam is aimed at whatever the holographic artist wants to be recorded. The light from the object beam scatters onto the holographic plate and, with the reference beam, creates an interference that "photographs" the image.

The Hologram Universe, one company that produces holographic images for NASA, Stanford University, Nissan, IBM, and others, asserts that "holography is part of the light age of information and communications: Holograms use light as a form of inkless printing, fiber optics will carry communications at the speed of light, optical computers will soon be a reality. Light is the future." Are we moving toward the Age of Light ... the Age of the Angels?

Holograms do produce images that float ethereally. If the holographic image advances toward you, it is *real*. If the image stands back, as if on the other side of an open doorway, it is called *virtual*. When the image is inside out, that's *pseudoscopic*. When it's right side out, it's *orthoscopic*.

Let's look at holograms as a human metaphor for approximating the Divine Light, a way to reflect, record, and interpret angel messages. Remember, each particle of light that makes up a hologram holds within it *everything* about the whole image, shown from that particle's unique point of view.

For this meditation, you'll need a candle, sandalwood incense (sandalwood is a fragrance long associated with the Divine and sacred sight, but you can use any incense fragrance you particularly like), a CD or audiotape of sitar or harp music, and a quiet, dark place. If you are outdoors, you might want to use the full moon as your light source instead of candlelight.

1. Light the incense as you prepare your space so the fragrance can begin to fill and infuse it, stimulating your senses and carrying your intent upward. Begin the music; you might want to listen on your iPod or portable CD player if you have one. Place your candle (unless the full moon is your guide) so that its flame will be clearly visible to you at your eye level when you are seated comfortably cross-legged in meditation pose on the ground or on the floor.

2. Sit in meditative pose and breathe slowly and deeply, inhaling and exhaling until you are one with the music. Focus your vision on the candle flame or on the moon's orb, allowing yourself to be drawn into the light, to become one with it.

3. As your conscious hearing mind, your sensate body, and your yearning spirit merge with the light, take a deep breath in and hold it. With the exhale, whisper out loud a word or a name associated with some issue or situation on which you are requesting clarification. Allow the sound and breath to vibrate into the light.

4. Now, perceive an angel of light traveling toward you from the light, reaching out to touch you. The angel is *real* and carries to you the quality you must nurture to understand the angel message surrounding your situation. As the angel reaches you, feel yourself bathed in celestial light. Breathe in deeply and hold it. With the

exhale, whisper the word for the quality this angel has delivered to you. Thank the angel for its blessing, and allow it to dissolve into the light.

5. Now, perceive an angel standing behind the light, beckoning to you. The angel is *virtual* and shows you the doorway you must pass through to understand the angel message surrounding your situation. Breathe in deeply and hold it. With the exhale, whisper the word for the doorway this angel has shown you. Thank the angel for its blessing, and allow it to dissolve into the light.

6. Now, perceive an angel emanating from the light and turning itself inside out, right side back, inside out, right side back, shape shifting. This angel is *pseudoscopic* and *orthoscopic* and reveals the heart of the matter surrounding your situation. Breathe in deeply and hold it. With the exhale, whisper the word that turns your situation inside out. Thank the angel for its blessing, and allow it to dissolve into the light.

7. To end this session, stretch out your arms, hands palm up, to either side, and take one full breath. As you exhale, repeat the word delivered by the first angel as you lift your hands over your head and bring your palms together. Continue to look into the light. Breathe in again deeply. With the exhale, repeat the word shown by the second angel as you lower your hands down before your heart in prayer pose. Continue to look into the light. Breathe in again deeply. With the exhale, repeat the word revealed by the third angel. Bow your head and close your eyes as you draw your angel answers deep into your core and ground your being with their Divine wisdom here on the earth plane.

Dreamtime

The oldest known object crafted intentionally as a musical instrument is the Australian didgeridoo, a hornlike instrument that originated with the aborigines (often characterized as the earth's "first people"). It emits a plaintive, resonant series of tones that vibrate through hollowed wood that the player can alter through breath control and percussion (tapping). For early aborigines, the didgeridoo was the voice of nature, the song of the spirits. Made from branches hollowed out by termites and scorched smooth by passing hot coals through the inside, the didgeridoo came from the earth, sounded like the wind, and summoned the gods.

Scientists who study ancient civilizations believe early aboriginal tribes used the didgeridoo's tones to evoke the trancelike state known as Dreamtime, an energy existence in which everything was everything. According to aboriginal mythology, plants, animals, humans, the stars and the planets, and the gods all could transform into each other—and did so freely. Dreamtime was The Beginning, the start of the earth's existence and the origins of humankind. As the earth's populations of plants and animals grew, differentiation increased, and slowly each form of existence lost the ability to change shape and form. Trees were trees, bears were bears, and humans, now on the scene as representations of the gods, were humans. The gods retreated to the heavens to live among the stars and the planets. Only when intentionally entering Dreamtime was it possible to again return to the oneness of The Beginning. The tones of the didgeridoo provided this passage.

The meditative state you entered as you performed the hologram meditation encourages you to experience something like entering Dreamtime as you manifested and shifted shape and form with your angels. Paradoxically, it is in these moments of oneness with the eternal that we find all our individual answers and insights. *In the beginning was the Word* … Even as you experience a Divine oneness, the particular beauty and uniqueness of each message is communicated with each word offered for your highest and best.

Light Works: Harmonize with the Angels

Still have your pitch pipe handy? Bring it out! Earlier, you discovered how to use a pitch pipe to create the single tones of each of the celestial chakra energies. Now you'll use the pitch pipe only to warm up your voice. Then, you'll string chant syllables together to create your own harmonic combinations for the angels. From now on, you can enter meditation with celestial music from your lips to the angel's ears.

Take several preparatory, cleansing breaths—breathe in through your nose one … two … three … four … five, and breathe out through your mouth one … two … three … four … five.

Using your pitch pipe, sound each of the higher chakra notes. Breathe in through your nose for the count of five, and breathe out through your mouth and the pitch pipe over the count of five.

B   Crown chakra

A   Third eye chakra

F#   Throat chakra

G#   Heart chakra

Now use your voice to sound each of the higher chakra chant tones. Again, breathe in through your nose for the count of five, then allow your vocal cords to make the sound of each chant tone as you breathe out over the count of five. Do all four tones, one at a time.

B   *Om*

A   *Ah*

F#   *Ham*

G#   *Yam*

Now put two chant tones together—any two. Sound one and then the other on successive breaths. Remember to breathe in through your nose for the count of five, then draw each chant note for the count of five as you breathe out. Write the tones and chant sounds you use:

Chant 1: _____

Chant 2: _____

Chant 3: _____

Practice until you like the way your tones sound. Also pay attention to what happens in your body and your mind as you chant. Do you feel yourself opening and becoming one with the Universe? Think of each tone as a symbol that represents an aspect of your message, a hologram of sound instead of light. Hear your voice as the sound your angel plucks on a rainbow harp of light.

When you are comfortable with your two-tone message, add a third tone. Work your way up to incorporating all four tones and then experiment with different combinations of tones.

You can create angel messages as complex as you like. Just remember to form intent around what you want each tone or combination of tones to represent. Write your combinations in your journal so you can keep track of them, like code sheets. Create combinations for health, prosperity, abundance, or whatever you desire the angels to help you with.

Light Works: Chapter 9 Angel Card

This chapter's angel card word is *Wisdom*. This card needs to show depth and breadth, the spectrum of knowledge and insight. Wisdom comes from so many directions but always from one Source. There is the learning of outer wisdom, the wisdom that others see in us. And there is the inner wisdom each of us has to help us connect with the wisdom of the Divine. Wisdom also evokes a sense of completeness. Using color, movement, and form, create your angel card for *Wisdom*.

Highest and Best: Virtual Mountain Climbing

Many spiritual writings and songs use the image of the mountain to depict getting closer to the Divine. Here is another meditation to help you climb to the higher realm.

1. Go to your sacred space or a place where you will not be disturbed. Prepare a question you would like answered. This is a good exercise to use to elaborate upon the angel words gifted to you in the hologram meditation. If possible, it would be best this time to pre-record the steps of this meditation and listen to your own voice as a guided meditation on tape or CD. Always surround yourself with a protective white light before you begin.

2. Start by taking three deep breaths in through your nose and out through your mouth, the first to clear your body, the second to open your mind, and the third to free your spirit.

3. Visualize that you are standing in the sunrise of a warm summer morning. The sky is brilliant with beautiful colors—glorious magenta and vivid orange.

4. See a mountain in the distance. Let it appear to you as it will, don't try to give it particular shape, height, or presentation.

5. Start walking toward the mountain; this is the mountain you will climb.

6. Continue to climb the mountain, which might appear to have smooth paths or be steep and rocky.

7. See a small waterfall and stop to play in it. Allow yourself to feel the waterfall and enjoy it as it presents to you.

8. Eventually decide to continue to climb until you get to the top.

9. When you get to the top, meet your angel or guide. Ask the question you prepared, and spend some time in discussion about the question and the circumstances it represents in your life. If you have also done the hologram meditation earlier in this chapter, discuss the angel words gifted to you and what importance each holds for resolving your question to the highest and best of all concerned.

10. Allow yourself to receive the answer.

11. Thank your guide or angel for what you have received and begin to climb down the mountain.

12. Pass the wonderful waterfall and remember the joy of playing in it.

13. Come back to the place you began, and enjoy the fulfilled feeling of receiving the answer you desired from your angel or guide.

When you return to the reality of your sacred place, take a few minutes to write in your journal about the experience of your virtual climb, your interaction with your angels and spirit guides, and the message you received.

What beauty, what joy, resides in affirming your connection to the Divine! When you chant, when you visualize, when you open yourself to both receive and give, you bring completeness to your own life as well as to the energy of the Universe. It is the energy of existence and the energy of empowerment. You are one ... and you are One.

Part 4

Working With Your Angels: Let Them In

Our angels can give us direction and let us know that we're on the right path—and they can let us know when we've created diversions that take us astray. The Kabbalah says that when we do wrong things it's because we are afraid of the Light. Sometimes we're afraid because of the responsibility of our paths and sometimes because, in our own humanness, we can't accept that these might be our paths. They are different from what we envision when we think about our reasons for our lives. Maybe your lifepath doesn't feel grand enough to make a difference, but know that every lifepath has a reason, every lifepath matters, and every lifepath makes a difference.

We *all* have our paths, and we have freewill that gives us many ways to travel toward the same destination—the Divine. Do you feel uncomfortable with your choices? Maybe that's the work of your angels, nudging you—and sometimes giving you a hefty shove—back onto your path. When you are uncertain or confused, call on your angels. They will always tell you what is true.

An angel is a belief with wings, and arms to carry you.
—Hannah Pitt (played by Meryl Streep) in *Angels in America* (2003)

Chapter 10

Manifesting With Angels

When we talk about manifesting with angels, we are talking about *bringing into being*. What you chose to manifest can be tangible or intangible—from coaxing a smile and a hug from your teenage son to offering a prayer for humanity's best destiny. It can be seemingly frivolous or obviously profound—from winning that eBay auction for a pair of never-worn Manolo Blahnik Mary Janes, Carrie Bradshaw's urban shoe myth in *Sex and the City,* to conceiving a child after many years of trying. Manifesting, in all its forms, is a sacred act of creation.

Whatever it is you are working to bring into being, know that your Divine Intent is legitimate and reasonable, whether the purpose is small, mundane, and practical or whether it looms large and feels overwhelming to accomplish. Remember that your intent in manifesting whatever you desire must be in reaching for the highest and best for yourself and for the people and spirits around you. With this rule in mind, you can be assured of the help of your angels and spirit guides in manifesting all that you need—just be prepared for some surprises and twists and turns on the journey!

Whether you are rewarded in this moment, today, with the object of your manifesting efforts or not (we don't *always* get everything handed to us on a silver platter by our angels and guides just because we want it!), you must understand that it is the process and purpose of manifesting, of bringing into being, that is most important. The act of creation moves us forward and compels us to continually reevaluate our lives, our relationships, and the circumstances that surround us. Manifesting asks us to strive for something better, brighter, and lighter for ourselves and for the ones we love.

As we envision our future, our dreams, and our goals for the next 10 minutes or the next 10 years, we engage in a continuum that actually stretches beyond time, distance, or space. We engage in an eternal angelic continuum of *becoming*. The ultimate act of becoming is our own enlightenment, our own returning to the Divine Source of All Understanding. *All* spirits on Earth and in the higher realm yearn for this return to the Source, including your angels and spirit guides, in whom and with whom you share your divinity, and from which source all is made manifest! Think about the angelic soul groups Elucia spoke of in Chapter 3 that merge and emerge from the Divine Light, where individuality and wholeness are energetically joined and lose their distinction as we know and understand that distinction of *self* and *whole* to be.

When we allow ourselves to follow the manifesting energy of the Universe toward the Source as an opening flower follows the warmth of the sun, we become open to the full potential of our essential being. *We know who we have been, we are who we want to be, and we become our highest and best.* Let's take a look at manifesting with the angels.

Light Works: Chapter 10 Angel Card

This chapter's angel card word is *Bliss*. When you have bliss, you are fulfilled. Abundance, in all the meanings it has for you, manifests all that fills your life. You are dynamic and engaged in the world around you. You are centered, content, and joyous. Bliss comes from within you. You want your angel card for *Bliss* to represent this manifestation of inner happiness. You might want to choose soft colors and forms to create a sense of gentle, flowing movement or bright, bold images that proclaim your joy.

Angels for Every Occasion and Purpose

There are hundreds of named angels in various sources from religious texts to secular writings. Numerous variations on spellings of angel names arise from the challenges of translating from the original languages of antiquity—perhaps a half-dozen or so languages through the millennia of civilization. The angel lists that follow represent names that I cross-referenced among multiple sources and angel traditions and chose the spellings that appeared most consistently. When you do your own angel research, you might encounter discrepancies; think "creative" when it comes to angel name spelling and pronunciation!

Even some angel names that we might not think today are related stem to similarities in the sounds of letters that predate written language. For example, you'll find Cassiel, angel of business endeavors and the planet Saturn, appears also as Casziel and Kafziel. And Sachiel, the angel of affluence as well as forgiveness, appears variably as Tzadkiel, Zedekiel, and Zadakiel. Metatron, patron angel of young children, is said to be known by more than 80 different names!

When you are manifesting with the angels, use this list to help guide you to the angel best suited for you to work with to achieve your purpose. Of course, the many angels and spirit guides who travel with you and are entrusted with your individual care and spiritual evolution are perhaps the *most* perfectly suited to work with *you* in manifesting your highest and best. But when it comes to Divine assistance, you can never have too many angels!

Angels of Change and Transformation
- **Colopatiron** liberation and freedom through intuition
- **Ezekiel** dynamic existence

Angels of Divine Intent
- **Seraphim** choir of angels that burn with Divine Love and connect us to its energy
- **Thrones** angels of justice and executors of the Will

Angels of Miracles
- **Hamied** Divine intervention
- **Melchisedek** leader of the Virtues
- **Michael** archangel of miracles, supreme guardian
- **The Virtues** choir of angels responsible for miracles

Angels of Health, Healing, and Forgiveness
- **Anael** health and longevity
- **Ariel** cure of disease
- **Azbuga** healing of illnesses and injuries
- **Baglis** overcoming addiction
- **Balthial** forgiveness
- **Gavreel** making peace and ending discord and arguments
- **Mumiah** vigor and longevity
- **Raphael** Divine healer
- **Sachiel** forgiveness
- **Sariel** healing and wholeness
- **Shekinah** emotional and spiritual balance

Angels of Patience, Grace, and Compassion
- **Ananchel** opens the heart to Divine love
- **Asmodel** patience and common sense
- **Barchiel** compassion
- **Chamuel** tolerance for others and love for self and others
- **Hael** kindness
- **Melchisedek** peace and righteousness
- **Ooniemme** gratitude and blessing
- **Rhamiel** empathy and understanding
- **Valoel** calmness, tranquility, and inner peace

Angels of Abundance, Prosperity, and Work
- **Anauel** achieving success and prosperity and sharing wealth
- **Barakiel** good fortune
- **Barbelo** prosperity and goodness
- **Cassiel** business endeavors
- **Maion** self-discipline and hard work
- **Michael** wealth and success
- **Perpetiel** victory and success
- **Sachiel** wealth, riches, affluence, and the ability to make money

Angels of Love, Joy, Friendship, and Partnership

- **Anael** romantic love, passion, and sexuality
- **Barakiel** playfulness and lightheartedness
- **Camael** beauty, joy, and gratification
- **Charmeine** harmony and joy
- **Gabriel** joy, love, and truth in communication
- **Hadraniel** Divine love
- **Mihr** friendship and business partnerships
- **Muriel** deep feelings and emotions
- **Ongkanon** truth in communicating deep feelings
- **Sammael** romance, passion, and marriage
- **Soqed Hozi** balances emotions and truth between intimate partners
- **Verchiel** affection and generosity

Angels of Family, Fertility, and Children

- **Anahita** fertility and fruitfulness
- **Ardoustus** childbirth and breast-feeding
- **Gabriel** pregnancy and guardian of souls waiting to enter the world
- **Lailah** conception

Angels of Learning, Truth, Wisdom, and Integrity

- **Ambriel** inner truth
- **Amitiel** learning that leads to truth and wisdom
- **Armaita** truth and wisdom of the heart
- **Bath Kol** prophecy
- **The Cherubim** choir of angels responsible for sacred lessons and knowledge
- **Dina** learning
- **Haamiah** ethics and enlightenment
- **Hamaliel** order and logic in thought
- **Harahel** new ideas and enlightenment
- **Jophiel** open-mindedness and inner vision
- **Mihael** loyalty, fidelity, and trustworthiness

- **Vohu Manah**   purity of thought
- **Zagzagel**   listening to the inner self and wisdom

Angels of Creativity, Inspiration, and Life Path
- **Afriel**   exploration and discovery
- **Anahita**   bringing ideas to fruition
- **Ecanus**   writing
- **Gabriel**   vision of the Third Eye
- **Gazardiel**   spiritual awakening and enlightenment
- **Liwet**   inventiveness and original ideas
- **Micah**   spiritual evolution and growth on life path
- **Raphael**   creativity, intuition, and the arts
- **Samandiriel**   imagination and visualization
- **Uriel**   artistic passion and creative vision
- **Vohamanah**   optimism

Angels of Faith, Hope, Courage, and Strength
- **Abdiel**   faith in the face of adversity
- **Barchiel**   inner strength
- **Machidiel**   spiritual courage
- **Rampel**   strength and endurance
- **Sandalphon**   courage, strength, and balance
- **Uzziel**   faith and inner strength

Angels of Human Endeavor

For many of us, what we *do* defines who we *are*. The search for the right work in this life journey is a major focus of struggle and concentration for a lot of people, and maybe it is for you, too. Even if you have found your calling and know what kind of work is the right work for you, the path to manifesting what you want to do might not seem exactly clear or achievable. These days, most of us will change our work many times in the course of our life paths. Or you might find yourself wishing to manifest very specific work goals, unique to the path you are firmly launched upon. To these ends, we look to the patron angels who watch over each of the professions. These angels guide and assist us in all our human endeavors to build community and nurture Divine understanding in human experience.

Patron Angels

- **Cassiel**   investors, stock brokers, and gamblers
- **Ecanus**   writers
- **Gabriel**   sailors and travelers
- **Israfel**   musicians, singers, and composers
- **Jophiel**   artists
- **Michael**   police officers and soldiers
- **Metatron**   young children
- **Raphael**   doctors, nurses, scientists, writers, artists, and teachers
- **Sachiel**   those with affluence and power
- **Sammael**   soldiers, politicians, and lawyers
- **Uriel**   those working with literature and music

If a man is called to be a streetsweeper, he should sweep streets even as Michelangelo painted or as Beethoven composed music or Shakespeare wrote poetry. He should sweep streets so well that all the hosts of heaven and earth will pause to say, here lived a great streetsweeper who did his job well.
—Martin Luther King Jr. (1929–1968), American civil rights leader

Your Guardian Angel

Of course, we are all familiar with the concept of guardian angels, angels whose job it is to look after us. Our guardian angel, according to many traditions, is assigned to our individual care. Guardian angels can be powerful facilitators, such as 600-winged Djibril, Islam's name for Gabriel, the angel through whom the words of the Koran were given to Muhammad, or the mighty-voiced Hadraniel who helped guide Moses to the Torah. Our guardian angels are often the keepers of, or the gateway to, Divine words and understanding.

In Frank Capra's classic American film *It's a Wonderful Life,* Clarence Oddbody, Angel Second Class, gives the classic American book, *Tom Sawyer,* to his charge, George Bailey. In the book, Clarence writes, "Remember, *no* man is a failure who has friends. Thanks for the wings!" By helping George gain a new appreciation for his life's worth, Clarence becomes a full-fledged angel with a full pair of wings. Clarence is perhaps not so grand as Djibril or as thunderous as Hadraniel, but he is a powerful angelic force for one man's goodness—and so to all whom his Divine humanity touches as well.

Do you believe there is one guardian angel who is assigned to nudge, prompt, cajole, coax, and protect *you?* If you said yes, you might be happy to know that there are *many* such guardian angels in your life, both on the earth plane and in the spirit realm. Together, every spirit forms a tapestry of Divine intent and healing protection that vibrates around you and connects you to all human beings and beings of Spirit. In other words, we are our own and each other's guardian angels in an ever-expanding network of grace—as Clarence Oddbody would affirm, a community of friends!

Do we always *listen* to our guardian angels and heed their advice and wisdom? Maybe, even though we might not *believe* we are .... We know one old Italian grandmother who regularly used her cane to beat away her guardian angel whenever the angel drew too close. "Go away, I know who you are but I'm not going with you!" she'd shout as she gave her guardian the boot. When asked if she was worried that the angel would be offended, this grandmother replied with a chuckle, "God knows I'm ornery. It's no surprise!"

This was a wise response, for we all wrestle with our guardian angels, as our human will grapples at its intersection with manifesting our highest and best. Angels know we are sometimes our own worst enemies, clinging to our very human natures even as we recognize their Divine presence in our midst. Perhaps the message of this guardian angel for this grandmother was to affirm the old woman's faith and engagement in living, in being alive on the earth plane and relishing every moment of her 90-plus-years life journey.

When was the last time *you* felt the presence of a guardian angel in your experience? I love asking this question of the people I meet through my Spirit ministry. Everyone has a wonderfully rich story to tell. Did you welcome your guardian angel, or did you wrestle your angel for its blessing? Write the story of your guardian angel here:

My guardian angel and I _____

_____

_____

_____

I have a wonderful friend and colleague, Neal Ryder, who is a gifted radiant healer. I did a spirit drawing for Neal, and by my hand was revealed a wise spirit teacher with amazing warmth and energy who stands with Neal and guides him in his healing work.

Neal Ryder's guardian angel of healing Spirit being.

An Angel for Any Time

Traditionally, every month, day, and even hour has an angel assigned to it. (See Appendix A to work with the Angels of the Hours.) With such celestial support and oversight, you are *always* in the company of angels. Call on the Angels of the Months or the Angels of the Days for extra support with concerns or difficulties you're having in a particular angel's realm of expertise, or ask the angels to provide general protection and guidance.

Angels of the Days

- **Sunday** Michael, overseer of all angels
- **Monday** Gabriel, bearing focus on nurturing, creativity, pregnancy, and childbirth
- **Tuesday** Sammael, bearing focus on emotional passion
- **Wednesday** Raphael, bearing focus on healing, travel, and communication
- **Thursday** Zachariel, bearing focus on surrender
- **Friday** Anael, bearing focus on passion and sexuality
- **Saturday** Cassiel, bearing focus on social order, temperance, and the planet Saturn

Angels of the Months

- **January** Gabriel, bringing news and new beginnings
- **February** Barakiel, bringing benevolence
- **March** Machidiel, bringing fortitude and boldness
- **April** Asmodel, bringing patience and sensibility
- **May** Ambriel, bringing protective guidance
- **June** Muriel, bringing emotional expression and awareness
- **July** Verchiel, bringing generosity and splendor
- **August** Hamaliel, bringing orderliness and structure
- **September** Zuriel, bringing harmony and peace
- **October** Barakiel, bringing good fortune
- **November** Adnachiel, bringing honesty and openness
- **December** Hamael, bringing grace and dignity

Again you might notice that many of these angels have multiple realms of influence. Once you become familiar with the range of an angel's oversight, you can call on combinations of angels to guide, comfort, or protect you with great specificity. The more specific you are, the more likely you are to manifest and receive what you expect and desire for your highest good. If you know that an important upcoming event will happen during a specific month or on a specific day, you can use the guardian angels of that month and day to enhance the energy and work toward manifesting a beneficial outcome. You can even look at the angel energy of a particular day *before* scheduling something important so the energy of the event resonates with angelic harmony.

Of course, sometimes the angels know better than we do about what kind of energy we need. Know that the Angels of the Days and the Angels of the Months are *always* using their Divine energy on your behalf, as is our constellation of personal guardian angels and spirit guides. None of us has the luxury of time to consciously work with angelic energies hour after hour day after day, so we must trust their constant intercession and remember that the Divine is always working for the best to manifest. (Even though it might not seem that way when your cell phone falls out of your purse and you run over it with the car, the dog won't poop for anyone but you, no one can figure out why the computer *refuses* to connect to the Internet, and your teenage daughter is giving you advice on the correct way to wear a thong! Take heart, even these moments are Divine.) Look back to the techniques I've given you in previous chapters for connecting to Eternal Spirit and how to access and hold the Divine within you even as you move through your daily adventures, and remember you are blessed!

By the Compass

Especially on those days when you need to find your way, fine-tune your internal compass by turning to these angels as signposts to put you back on your proper path. Wiccan practitioners invoke the Angels of the Directions when putting up a magick circle.

Angels of the Directions

- **Raphael** East
- **Gabriel** West
- **Uriel** North
- **Michael** South

In the Light: The Angel of Your Birth *Day*

Do you know what *day* of the week you were born on? This day marks the angel of your birth, a special angelic guide and guardian. If you don't know what day you were born, you can look it up using a perpetual calendar (a compendium that lists calendars back and ahead in time); libraries usually have these. Find the calendar for the year, month, and date of your birth, which will show you the day of the week you were born. There are also online versions; type *perpetual calendar* into your web browser. Once you know your day of birth, find the corresponding angel from the previous Angels of the Days list.

The Angel of Your Birth Day gives you added strength in the area the angel oversees. How can you use the attributes of your special angel to guide and encourage you in your daily life? Make a list of the things you do every day and ways you can enlist the support of your birth day angel. When you find yourself engaged in one of those activities, take a moment to ask:

Angel of my birth, angel of my day, guide my decisions and actions for the highest and best.

Angels of the Zodiac

You probably can answer in a heartbeat the question, "What's your sign?" Most of us know at least this much of astrology, our natal or sun signs. But do you know your *Zodiac Angel?* Until the Middle Ages, astrology and angels shared equal weight in the belief systems of Eastern and Western cultures alike. Astrology was the science of the heavens, and Heaven was the home of the angels—a natural connection. Each of the original 7 planets (those planets plus the Sun and the Moon discovered before powerful telescopes made it possible to see to the edge of the Milky Way) and each of the 12 sectors, or signs, of the zodiac has a corresponding angel:

Angels of the Planets

- **Sun**   Raphael, angel of health and life
- **Moon**   Gabriel, angel of nurturing
- **Mercury**   Michael, angel of protection
- **Venus**   Anael, angel of romantic love

- **Mars** Uriel, angel of illumination
- **Jupiter** Zachariel, angel of releasing material attachments
- **Saturn** Cassiel, angel of solitude

Angels of the Zodiac
- **Aries** Machidiel, angel of courage
- **Taurus** Asmodel, angel of practicality
- **Gemini** Ambriel, angel of inner truth
- **Cancer** Muriel, angel of emotions
- **Leo** Verchiel, angel of generosity
- **Virgo** Hamaliel, angel of logic and order
- **Libra** Zuriel, angel of harmony
- **Scorpio** Barakiel, angel of lightning
- **Sagittarius** Adnachiel, angel of independence
- **Capricorn** Hamael, angel of persistence
- **Aquarius** Cambiel, angel of unconventional thought
- **Pisces** Barakiel, angel of compassion

And yes, you do see the same angel—Barakiel—assigned to both Scorpio and Pisces, although with a different designation. (In some resources, you'll see Barakiel assigned to Scorpio and Barbeil assigned to Pisces. Most angel systems consider these variations on spelling for the same angel.) Many angels have more than one dominion, or realm of influence, and Barakiel happens to pull double duty in the zodiac.

In the Light: Angelic Astrology

The cornerstone of astrology is the horoscope wheel, a circle divided into 12 sections or houses. Each house represents a specific dimension of one's life and has a natural zodiac sign affiliation. The following illustrations show the horoscope wheel, its houses, and their natural signs.

The natural planets and natural signs reside in their astrological houses.

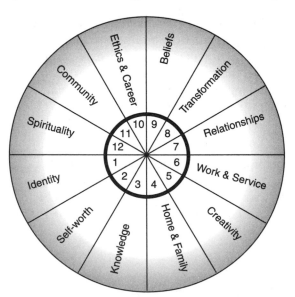

Each astrological house has manifesting energies for your life.

As heavenward stargazers have done for centuries, you can combine your angelic and astrological influences to increase your understanding of the events and circumstances surrounding your life as well as to choose actions that can lead you to manifest personal growth and evolve spiritually.

For example, is your teenager creating turbulence within your family? Family is in astrology's 4th house, the venue of Cancer. Muriel, the angel of emotional expressiveness, shares this house. Invoke the guidance of Muriel to tame those adolescent outbursts ... and to temper parental reactions. Looking for a new job? Work and career reside in the 6th house under the natural sign of Virgo. Sharing residence here is the angel Hamaliel, who brings orderliness and structure. Ask Hamaliel to help you organize your approach to manifesting the job you desire so you can go about it in an efficient, effective manner.

In what areas of your life would you like an angelic boost? Identify the astrological house and its corresponding sign and angel, and ask for the assistance you desire! Use the illustration and the lists of signs and angels, and fill in the following request:

I want to manifest _____
a function of the _____ house. The sign _____
naturally resides in this house along with the angel _____

Remember to make your requests specific and for the highest and best, and be open to receiving your answers and angel messages in unexpected ways.

Tarot's Angels

Traditional Tarot decks, such as the Universal Waite Tarot Deck, contain images of three of the archangels (and one notorious fallen angel ...) within its 22 Major Arcana cards, the karma or destiny cards, of the deck. You can use these Tarot cards to perform angel divination meditations to gain further insights into the energy you want to manifest with and through your angels.

Major Arcana Tarot Card	Angel	Meaning
The Lovers (VI): *Use this card to manifest harmony in relationships and good partnership.*	Raphael	The angel of air blesses the couple who stands before the Tree of Knowledge and Tree of the Zodiac.
Temperance (XIV): *Use this card when you need to cultivate balance and patience in your manifesting efforts.*	Michael	The angel of fire stands balanced between water and Earth, pouring Divine essence between the cup of the conscious and the cup of the subconscious.
The Devil (XV): *Use this card to remember that whatever you desire to manifest must be for your highest and best to avoid obsessive or destructive behaviors and habits.*	Lucifer, the fallen angel	Upright, this dark angel rules over obsession and material greed. Reversed, or upside down, this devil's angel clothes begin to show as the couple finds release from obsessive thinking and the chains that bind.
Judgement (XX): *Use this card to rejoice in manifesting a Divine connection to your angels and spirit guides.*	Gabriel	The angel of water, awakens the Divine essence in each human spirit with a trumpeting call to joy.

There are many, many Tarot decks to choose from that contain beautiful drawings and allegorical depictions of angels. These can inspire and provoke you to new understandings and realizations if you are interested in further incorporating the ancient divination tool of the Tarot into your angel sessions. I've included a few of my own paintings of Tarot's Major Arcana cards in this book, and for me, the Tarot represents a powerful and insightful visual medium for self-exploration and for gaining insights into manifesting dreams and desires, much like The Hermit, shown here. As you do readings and work with the cards, remember that your angels can send you messages through the Tarot, too!

Rita's painting of Tarot's Major Arcana card The Hermit *lights the path to manifesting insights and deep spiritual truths with your angels and spirit guides.*

Cupid: Calling On the Angel of Love

Of all the things we humans attempt to manifest, perhaps the most universal is love. When it comes to manifesting true love, of course, whom else should you call on but Cupid? The mischievous winged cherub, bow and arrow at the ready, arises from ancient Roman mythology in which Cupid was the son of Venus, the goddess of love and beauty, and the god Jupiter. The premise of Cupid, who "shoots" arrows of love and passion into (mostly unsuspecting) lovers, permeates legend and lore across cultures—Shakti the energy of sensual passion in Hinduism, the lusty god Kane of Polynesian mythology, the Japanese goddess of eroticism Rati. In early Christianity, Cupid made the transition from myth to guardian spirit responsible for steering young men in the direction of love.

Cupid's reputation for fun and pranks underlies the tradition of the secular celebration of St. Valentine's Day, the annual day of lovers. Call on Cupid to infuse this day with passionate adventure for you and your partner or to help you meet the partner of your dreams. Look to the unexpected when you summon Cupid; he will bring you what you ask for, although often in a manner not quite what you had in mind. From instant infatuation to quarrelers-turned-lovers, the arrow of Cupid tends to strike fast and fierce with the intention of creating long-lasting love.

A Love Story

Sometimes things just blurt out of your mouth that are very important angel messages for the person you're talking to. When Charlotte was 18 or so, she broke up with a young man, Louis, and accepted a date with a new guy, Dennis. Then Louis sent Charlotte roses and poetry, and she found herself telling Dennis she had to go back to Louis and give it another try—hey, she was young! When Charlotte told her friend Chloe about this turn of events, Chloe gave an unexpected response. She said, "But maybe Dennis is the man you're going to marry. How do you know if you don't let it unfold?"

Chloe's question turned out to be prophetic. Things did not work out with Louis—not surprisingly as the relationship had been rocky for much of its existence. Chloe's words stuck in Charlotte's mind but as time passed Charlotte figured she'd never see Dennis again and eventually put him out of her thoughts. About two years after her breakup with Louis, Charlotte answered the phone one evening to find Dennis on the other end. This time the connection was clear, and they've been together every day since. Chloe's angel words came home to Charlotte's heart!

Cupid's moral for this love story: Roses and poetry are great when you get them from the right guy! In other words, look deeply for Cupid's message (and for that matter, *any* angelic message); it might be deeper and subtler than what it appears on the surface.

In the Light: Relationship Remedies

When it comes to love and romance, many other angels join Cupid in his matchmaking efforts. Looking to spark your love interest or deepen your relationship? Call on …

- **Anael** to infuse your relationship with romantic love, passion, and sensual pleasure
- **Barakiel** for playful, lighthearted fun
- **Charmeine** to head off or turn the corner on lover's quarrels
- **Gabriel, Muriel, and Ongkanon** to help you express the truth and depth of your emotions
- **Hadraniel** to deepen the bond between partners and the Divine energy of love
- **Sammael** when you're ready to take your relationship to the threshold of marriage or to spice things up within your marriage
- **Soqed Hozi** to help you balance, in loving kindness, your emotions and the truth in an intimate partnership
- **Verchiel** to find the perfect ways to express your generosity and affection toward your partner (and maybe a little help with those anniversary and Valentine's Day gifts, too!)

Call on one of these relationship angels each day to keep your partnership on course. Write the name of each angel and his or her realm of influence on a small card, and randomly choose a card each morning (or evening!). Ask these angels to work with your guardian angels and spirit guides to manifest the true expression of love every being of Spirit craves and deserves.

Light Works: This Is Your Life!

Have you every played the popular board game *Life?* In this game, the wheel of chance tells you how far to move along the winding path of "Your Life." Each step of the path has instructions for certain life events—college, marriage, children, buying a home, etc.

What would the path of your life look like if you were to chart it out? Gather together a large piece of poster board and some markers or pens, and let's do just that! We'll look for the special manifesting influence of our angels and guides along our way.

1. On a large piece of poster board, make a starting point at the left edge of the paper, in the center, and label it with your date of birth.

2. Along the bottom of the board, create a scale that represents the years of your life. You can do this by decade, in increments of two or three or five years, or even one year at a time.

3. Draw lines up to the top edge of the board, like grid lines. Label the lines with the increment you've chosen. At the appropriate points, write in highlights from your life. Did you have an amazing birthday party when you were three? Draw a cake at that point on your grid.

4. Begin drawing a line—your life line—from the starting point (your birth) across the page. Fill in the highlights along your life's path. What angels might have influenced the decisions that manifested those highlights? Draw a pair of angel wings on your life line wherever you know your life path has crossed that of an angel.

5. Going forward, whenever you create a new affirmation or send a special request to your angels and guides, mark that point on your timeline with another set of angel wings.

6. Keep your life path chart in a safe place where you can come back to it to add the events that happen to you as your life follows its course. Continue to record the influence of angels along the way as you recognize their presence and manifesting work.

Are the events of your life consciously affected by what you put out to your angels and guides as dreams and goals you wanted to manifest? Did they turn out as you anticipated? If not, how are they different? Use your life chart to keep track of your dreams and desires and the many ways in which your angels and guides help you make them your reality.

Manifesting Angel Flags

There are many ways we can manifest thoughts, prayers, and energy with our angels and spirit guides. The Tibetan Buddhist tradition, extending back thousands of years to ancient cultures in China and India, uses prayer flags for health and longevity to send energy messages of personal and global healing into the Universe. The colors, symbols, and words on the flags shape their manifesting intent. Traditionally, flags appear in sets of five, one each of the elemental colors yellow, green, red, white, and blue. These are the colors of the environment (earth, water, fire, air, and space) as well as of the body. To make a set of angel prayer flags for manifesting, you need five squares, all the same size, of fabric in the elemental colors (yellow, green, red, white, and blue) and permanent markers or fabric paints so you can write and draw on the fabric. You also need enough medium-weight cord to fasten the flags together like a banner and glue or needle and thread to attach the flags to the cord.

1. Invite your guides and angels to join you, and ask that your combined energies unite to manifest your intent. Ask for blessing of your purpose and that it should be only in the service of the highest and best.

2. As you begin making your flags, visualize what you need to create or fulfill. This can be something you desire to manifest for yourself or to manifest in an aspect of your life such as a relationship or your career. You can also create the angel flags with the more general manifesting intent of increasing Divine energy and Spirit for the benefit of all humanity.

3. On each fabric square, write a word associated with what is to be manifested. You can write the same word or a different word on each square. You can write the word in the center of the flag or along any or each of the edges. You can write on both sides if the fabric is thick enough that the words won't show through.

4. If you like, draw images or designs on each flag that symbolize your intent. You can be as simple or as complex as you desire, as long as you retain your focus on the manifesting energies you want the flags to convey.

5. Fasten the flags together along the tops or the sides to form a banner. Always keep the colors in the traditional order of yellow, green, red, white, and blue.

6. Thank your guides and angels for the work you do together.

Hang your flags outside, where the wind will catch the energy of your manifesting angel message and carry it upward. If your flags are meant for you, you can hang them where you will see them often, whether indoors or outdoors. If your angel flags are meant to manifest something for the community or for humanity, place your angel flags outdoors where their prayers can be borne on the wind to touch as many lives as possible. Once you release your manifesting energy to the Divine, see whatever is needed as fully created and so Divine will be done.

Highest and Best: The Thousand-Petaled Lotus Blossom

Traditionally, angels wear halos of Divine energy surrounding their heads with heavenly Light. In Eastern thought, the crown chakra, the energy center that resides at the top of your head, blossoms as the thousand-petal lotus blossom. In previous chapters, we've evoked the lotus blossom when we talked about spiritual unfoldment, using the visual of a flower unfolding, opening to receive the visions and messages from our angels and the higher side, then closing petal by petal to ground us once again on the earth plane.

Something opens our wings. Something makes boredom and hurt disappear. Someone fills the cup in front of us: We taste only sacredness.
—Rumi (1207–1273), Sufi mystic poet

The ancient poet and mystic Rumi wrote of the lotus blossom with its roots in the mud and its spectacular flower blossoming above the water's rim. As we discussed at the start of this chapter, each act of manifestation is an act of Divine creation. Here in human form, we strive to connect our earthly roots to our aspirations for manifesting a Divine blossoming. I'd like to give you this guided meditation on the lotus blossom to help you unfold, opening yourself to the strength and beauty of manifesting with your angels, of *bringing into being, of Divine becoming.* (If you prefer, read this meditation into a tape recorder and play it back for your guided meditation or have someone else read it so you can immerse yourself in the experience.)

1. Sit cross-legged on a firm surface with your back erect. Relax your muscles, and feel your being align with both the gravity of the earth plane and the lightness of the higher realm.

2. Breathing in through your nose and out through your mouth, take three deep cleansing breaths—the first to cleanse your body, the second to clear your mind, and the third to open your spirit.

3. In the dark of the night, visualize your legs rooting and growing tendrils from your toes to reach down into the soft mud that swirls at the bottom of the river of life. Meditate on the archangel Michael as he stands one foot on the earth and one on the water in Tarot's Temperance card, the card of patience and nurturing growth.

4. Breathe into the center of rooted being with confidence and joy. Allow your torso to float as a lotus reed sways in the river of life.

5. In the light of dawn, spread your arms outward, palms facing the sun, and embrace the growing light as it flowers between your hands in an arc that unfolds petal by petal, a thousand brilliant petals of light emanating upward from your heart center, through your Third Eye, to create a crown of fragrant blossoms bursting open above the water's edge.

6. Breathe into the lightness of the lotus blossom that floats upward to the Divine.

7. Allow all the Divine light to enter your entire being, traveling deep into the rooted watery darkness below, infusing all with a celestial glow. Stay in that light and allow it to continue to enter as you connect to all there is.

8. You are a manifestation of the Divine. Say in your mind, *I blossom in the Divine Light.*

9. Invite your spirit guides and angels to join you, to give you the visions and the knowledge that the higher side wants to share with you. Stay in this energy for as long as you like or until you feel you have received all your angels and guides have to share.

10. Let yourself slowly close, each petal slowly folding inward one by one, a thousand times. Feeling relaxed and complete, relax comfortably into your body. Curl your toes and draw them back up from the mud below onto Earth's terra firma. Become conscious of your breathing. Remain seated for a few moments until you are fully returned to awareness of your environment.

11. Give thanks for this manifestation of your Divine Light.

Be willing to seek what you desire, to ask for what you want—always framed within the context of what is highest and best. There are no dreams too small, no visions too large. Ask ... and be ready to receive. And remember, each step, each gift, leads to another. What seems the impossible dream just might become your everyday life!

Chapter 11

Healing With Angels

The wings of angels wrapped around us possess a profound power to heal. Like the mother who kisses her child's scraped knee, there is no better antiseptic than love. We can release our pain to the angels. We can heal emotional scar tissue. We can be made whole. Whether the healing we seek is for physical, emotional, or spiritual pain, the healing guides and angels are there. They await to serve as guides through prolonged illnesses or be beacons of light on new life paths such as long-distance moves, new marriages, or departures of loved ones through death or divorce. Angels bring comfort and relief to chronic pain. They bring the light to darkness—old traumas, emotional pain rooted in childhood, mistakes we've made, damaged relationships, broken dreams, etc.

In my church we perform many healings calling on the power of angels and Spirit. The healing energy is so powerful because we call for the assistance of the Divine while in a Divine setting. People seek healing for a variety of reasons, some very concrete and tangible, such as the obstacles and limitations of dyslexia. But many of the healings address underlying emotions—fear, anxiety, depression, grief—that might or might not be consciously connected to a tangible event or cause.

As a healer, I ask that the energy of angels flows through me to the person to affect whatever kind of healing needs to occur for that person—and *I feel the Divine energy move through me*—and shift as it meets and ministers to the one who needs healing. Often, a healing takes place with the person sitting in a chair with the healer standing behind. Some healers feel as if they are being led to move their hands over certain areas of the person's body. There can be physical contact but it is not necessary; the healing that takes place is *energetic*. Many people experience immediate relief from symptoms such as headaches or back pain, but just as many experience a continuing healing that brings deep wounds, sometimes stored for years, to the surface. Often in the days or weeks after a healing, people will experience a profound release.

Why We Heal With Angels

To connect with the Divine we call upon our angels and healing guides for help. With their Light to embrace us we feel safe, comforted, and unconditionally loved. The power of unconditional love to promote healing transcends all other powers. In the safety and sanctity of that setting, we can release old fears that have lingered in our hearts, our bodies, our minds for many months or years. By their very nature, angels can restore our innocence—that is, *remind* us of our innocence by holding it out before us in their strong hands, sheltered in their gentle wings. They are a channel to purity and lightness. Ultimately, the healing energy of angels reminds us that we are not alone; we are not separate from each other or the Divine. We are one.

The healing comes in the shift of energy that reorders our perception. That shift from pain to purity, from separateness to connection, is a gift of Divine love.

> The voices of angels come to us in many ways—they come on quality wings of tenderness and healing; beauty and rekindled wonder, wings of healing and hope; comfort and kindness. Their verdict is always innocent; their sentence is always love.
> —Karen Goldman, *Angel Voices*

In the Light: Violet Flame

Often, in healing sessions, those who are sensitive to colors and are open to seeing auras experience a change in light. Both healer and receiver can experience this light energy shift. Sometimes aura connections are seen or photographed between healer and receiver. When healing for the session is taking place, often there is an influx of white light.

Try this exercise as a way to connect to the Divine healing energies of all angels in your life—angels from heaven, spirit guides, or earthly angels. After trying it once, you might want to read it aloud into your tape recorder to use as a regular meditation. Begin the first time by stating the intention:

I want to feel the purity and innocence of the Divine healing energy of my angels.

Your aim this first time is to gain a sense for what this feels like. On subsequent meditations, you might begin by stating a specific intention of an area of your life to which you would like to bring healing. As a hologram fills with light, as an angelic being *is* light, imagine the light of Divine healing energy entering your body and filling and illuminating your spirit.

1. Seated in a cross-legged or lotus position if possible or a seated position on with your back as straight as possible on a chair, take in three deep, cleansing breaths, in through your nose and out through your mouth. The first breath is to clear your body. Release it. Take a second breath to open your mind. Take a third breath to free your spirit.

2. Hold a violet crystal (amethyst) cupped in your hands before you to symbolize your crown chakra and your desire to connect to the healing energy of the Divine.

3. As you meditate with this crystal, imagine deep within you a deep violet flame. Breathe several minutes through this image in your mind until you feel it has become essentially integrated into you.

4. Now imagine the flame sending swirls of violet around your body, swirling upward to your crown, creating a pyramid of color and light. Breathe through this as you sense the color and light swirling upward on your body. Feel the movement of the energy.

5. When it feels complete, imagine this light transforming to white as it swirls to the top of the pyramid. Imagine the violet light giving way to the pure white light. Sit, breathe, and feel yourself enfolded in that purest of lights.

Afterward, as you progress on your specific healing, you might find it helpful to carry the amethyst crystal with you as a reminder that you have dedicated yourself to healing with the angels.

Calling the Priestess: The Role of Intuition

Your greatest ally in healing with angels is your intuition. Intuition is your inner knowing, the truth that guides you and opens you to the angel connection, the part of you that knows what you cannot yet see. It has as its seed your own innate sense that there is a benevolent presence in your life, bringing you comfort and wisdom. Your daily conversations and encounters with angels will continue to enhance your intuition.

As an artist, I find the image of the High Priestess represents the heightening of intuition. As one of the archetypes depicted in the Tarot, the High Priestess symbolizes the gaining of inner knowledge on the journey of life. She encourages us to trust in those truths we already know and guides us to pursue deeper truths within, yet to be uncovered.

Rita's painting invoking The Priestess, *from the Tarot's Major Arcana.*

The High Priestess is another form of angel guide, informing us about our wellness and bringing our bodies, minds, and spirits into alignment. Intuition is the voice inside us, the Divine speaking to us using our body's voice to inform us about the places where pain resides, pointing to the places we need to release and heal. Divine intuition points us to the path of faith, to step ahead when we don't yet see the light. It leads us to the place where miracles can happen, the clearing in the woods where the magical sword awaits. The angels are already there.

Miraculous Healing

When we speak of miraculous healing, we are speaking of healing that might defy intellectual understanding. We are not limited to the physical cures. The Divine sends angels to us to heal body, mind, and spirit. Such healing might come in the form of physical healing, yes, but it might just as easily come in the form of healing strained relationships, breaking through the logjam of years of misunderstandings and hurts to lift the relationship to a new plane. This is the tenderness of angels at work. They remind us how to forgive. They gently nudge us to alternative viewpoints to shift our perceptions.

In her song "Adia" (on the same album as "Angel"), singer/song-writer Sarah McLachlan sings of buying back her innocence as she mourns a broken relationship. As she contemplates her failures, she mourns their innocence (*"we are still innocent"*) just as much as the end of the relationship. Angels guide us again in seeking the path to a renewed, wiser innocence.

Light Works: Reconciliation

Is there someone in your life whom you seek healing with—a spouse who has grown emotionally estranged, a parent from whom you have distanced yourself, a friend who has judged you harshly? Is there someone you have stung with angry words that you would give anything to take back? Is there someone of whom you would like to ask forgiveness?

In previous chapters, we've asked you to draw mandalas as a way to connect to your angels. Here we will help you call on your healing angels by doing a sand painting mandala to reconcile a damaged relationship. In Tibetan monasteries, sand mandalas are designed in meditation over a period of weeks. They are arranged in intricate designs of colored sand, only to be swept away once completed. The aim of a sand painting mandala is not the result itself, but the process. It is your own inner process as you create your angel mandala of reconciliation that is the goal. Let your dialogue with angels working within be the journey that transforms you. The intensity of focus it takes to create such an intricate design will bring forward any messages from your angels in what in this relationship must transform to allow healing to occur. The temporal nature of the sand painting mandala serves to remind us that old hurts we hang on to are meant to be felt only temporarily, that they must be transformed through grace and forgiveness.

You might find a variety of fine-grain colored sands at a hobby shop or on the Internet. Choose found objects such as shells, milagros or charms, snapshots of yourself and the person you seek healing with, beads, stones, and other mementos. Find a place where you can work on your sand painting over a period of a week or two without it being disturbed.

For inspiration and ideas, you might want to turn to one of the many books of collected famous mandala patterns from cultures throughout time. One we can recommend is *Mandalas for Power and Energy* by Marion and Werner Küstenmacher. Some mandala patterns are available on the Internet, such as www.mandalaproject.org, which posts mandala drawings from people from all over the world.

Begin by meditating on your intent. Let your angels guide you in creating a melody of form. It is said that if two curved lines meet, they should approach each other until they merge; remember this as you draw your lines. This basic principle is found everywhere in nature: We are all connected. Like the leaf and the flower, like sky and Earth, like yin and yang, we ultimately become one. As you design your mandala, let that dynamic guide you—in strong lines that become thin lines and thicken again, in shapes that bloom, swell, fall, and fade. Let the melody of your heart lead you forward. Listen to its refrain; harken to how your angels answer back. Let each variation resound in your heart. As you do, the angels will open your heart to see the ways in which you and your estranged one are more alike than different. As you do, ask your angels to show you compassion for this person. Ask them to show you those times when he or she was crying out for love, when he or she was just as afraid as you were. Ask them to let the lines merge.

Someone Will Guide You

Angels are there to help us through times of need. They await us on the path, ready to be of service. Sometimes they come from surprising places. Sometimes they show up before we know we need them.

One night as I was sitting in a spirit communication circle at church, a student medium who rarely brings forth messages said she had received word from a woman whose surname was Jacobs. She described her as a small woman who lived in a small house, who worked very hard, and who loved others. She had dark skin and straight hair. "She is with you, and she brings lots of love," was the only message the student medium received.

I had a dear friend I helped through her battle with breast cancer. She would invite me to her home to give her healings after the people from her church left. The last time I was with her before she was ready to pass, she asked for my earrings and requested to be buried wearing them. This was the first time she had come through from the higher side, so the visit really stuck in my mind.

Three weeks later, I found a lump in my right breast and was diagnosed with breast cancer. I was truly touched that Ma Jacobs came to let me know that she would be there returning the love and healing, helping me through my own battle with breast cancer, from which I did recover.

The miracle can come, too, in the form of making an unbearable situation more tolerable, restoring us to a peace within. In the film *Wings of Desire,* for instance, angels rush to the scene of a car accident and cradle a dying person in their arms. During one healing service, a man who had inoperable lung cancer stepped forward for healing. Three healers worked on him. He left thanking us for restoring him to peace and freeing him from pain. All three healers felt a profound intensity of energy moving through them to this man. They were struck with gratitude at being permitted to be the conduit for this man's healing process.

Healing can work from afar as well, through remote Reiki healing or absent Spiritualist healing when energy is redirected through intensive thought, prayer, and energy movement, or through prayer vigils that stretch across miles, linked by candle flames. Try it—it works! Light a candle for a friend who is weighing a big decision or troubled about a relationship. Notice how it brings your awareness back to your friend during the day—and the angels that link you together.

An Angel Hug in Brooklyn

After 18 years of living in New York City, Lee Ann decided to make the break and move to Maryland's Eastern Shore. (We met Lee Ann, her grandmother Jess, and her great-grandmother Vennera in Chapter 1; and we met Lee Ann's angelic being Committee in Chapter 3.) She looked forward to the move, but with New York in her blood, the prospect of leaving was a daunting emotional undertaking. In the bustle of the last few days—saying good-byes to friends, packing her belongings, and pulling all-nighters to finish work—doubt and exhaustion descended upon her. Was she doing the right thing? Would her business thrive?

One beautiful spring day in Brooklyn, Lee Ann was sitting on the steps of her landlord's Park Slope brownstone sipping tea. The house had an iron gate and small garden in the front. As she sat contemplating, *Will I be okay?* a man about eight years younger than herself rode by on a bike. He called out "Hey beautiful" in a way that was not obnoxious or threatening and made Lee Ann laugh out loud. When the man heard her, he wheeled his bike around and came up to the iron gate, activating all Lee Ann's carefully bred New Yorker defenses. But instead, he just started chatting with her about what a beautiful day it was and how lovely it was to enjoy a cup of tea. Twice while he talked to Lee Ann, he greeted people walking by on the sidewalk as though he knew them, receiving responses from them as though they knew him as well. Both were very different people—one an aging homeless man with a long white beard and tattered, stained clothes, the other an executive in a well-tailored suit.

After about five more minutes of conversation, the man said, "You need a hug. May I hug you?" Sensing her hesitation, he said, "Don't worry. You just need some loving energy, I think." Amazingly, Lee Ann let him hug her. He opened the iron gate and she met him at the bottom of the steps. As he hugged Lee Ann, their hearts pressed together. He held her with firm, light support for close to a minute. "That's better," he said, "for your heart." Then he jumped on his bike and rode off with a wave and a smile.

That week Lee Ann moved to Maryland. Ever since she has wondered if she'd met an angel cyclist and whether the homeless man and the passing executive were angels, too. She wondered if angels *do* move among us, nodding to each other in recognition as they pass. Still, what Lee Ann does know for sure is that she received a healing heart boost on that day—just when she needed it.

There is only one path in this world in which nobody can go except yourself. Do not ask where it leads! Follow it!

—Friedrich Nietzsche (1844–1900), German philosopher, scholar, and poet

The Way In

When we embark on the healing path, opening ourselves to the healing power of angels, spirit guides, and earthly angels, it is important to remember that there are no crooked paths. There are times when the stored pain continues to erupt like a volcano and the release can be profound and intense. But you are never alone. Keep your amethyst quartz from your violet flame meditation with you as a talisman to keep you mindful of the new steps you are taking to cultivate your intuition and seek your angels. In the end, you will be able to look back and see how angels lighted your path.

It is a bit like entering a labyrinth. In a labyrinth, we begin the path without seeing the way ahead, yet we sense its center. We navigate a labyrinth through our senses, through all the twists and turns. In this way, we are restored to an innocence—the innocence angels remind us we indeed possess. Beginning at this point of innocence, when we cannot see the way through, creates the space in our thoughts and feelings that allows angels entry, when we forget ourselves for a moment and do not hold too tightly to our pain.

Think for a moment about a time in your life when you said, *Let it be as it must be,* a time when you relinquished the outcome. Think back to the moment before you let go. Was there a moment when you softened? When you let yourself be smaller, less defended? When you trusted? That's when the angels flew into the doorway of your heart, filling you with light and love for your healing journey.

The labyrinth in and of itself is believed to be a great healing tool because it leads you on the winding path to a true center. Labyrinths show up in many other cultures and times, from the one in the cathedral in Chartres, France; to the corn field mazes in the American Midwest; to the whimsical "Alice in Wonderland" labyrinth in Dorset, England; the hedge labyrinth in Russborough, England; or the modern-day Grace Cathedral in San Francisco. Europe is dotted with medieval cathedrals with labyrinth mosaics and stone paths near the entrance like that in Chartres, around which a liturgical dance was performed at the Easter service.

The website for the Grace Cathedral (www.gracecathedral.org/labyrinth/newlocator/newdb/) includes a labyrinth finder that can help you locate a labyrinth near you, and other websites offer labyrinth designs you can replicate in your backyard. The Labyrinth Society site (www.labyrinthsociety.org) includes a labyrinth finder, labyrinth designs, and instructions for making your own.

The Chartres Cathedral labyrinth invites you to take a healing walk with your angels to the Divine Source.

The labyrinth is linked to the mandala as a Western expression of the form. (In fact, there is a mandala in the rose window in the cathedral in Chartres.) Both represent the journey to the center. A classic labyrinth is distinguished from a maze, with its many forks, because a labyrinth has a closed circular path. When you walk it, you are forced to walk multiple outer paths traveling around the center. Only when you have experienced all dimensions of the labyrinth—metaphorically, all the dimensions of yourself—can you approach the center. So walking through the healing path of a labyrinth can be like retracing your steps to heaven. It can be disorienting. The labyrinth's path doesn't make apparent, logical sense—

and that's the point. The detours and wrong paths lead you to experience those truths that are difficult to access—that you might not otherwise have known.

Walking through a labyrinth with a partner is a metaphor for our walk with the angels. Imagine if you will, one person starting about 30 seconds ahead of the other. The second person enters just as the first turns the first corner. Both are walking the same path, yet the twists and turns bring you sometimes to walk side by side in the same direction, sometimes to meet and pass each other, sometimes on different sides of the labyrinth. Sometimes one is near the heart and the other at the rim. Sometimes it makes no sense what relationship you have to each other within the path. Still, you end up at the center together.

The walk with the angels can be like this—a dance of twists and turns, near and fear, known and perplexing. The Divine is always with us, coming and going—but in the end always arrives with us at the center, the Source of All Healing, rest, and joy.

Healing Places

I have a sacred place I go to in my mind when I meditate. I had a clear, vivid vision of it for many, many years. Then one day I found myself flipping through the pages of an old *National Geographic* from the 1950s and stopped on a photo that felt familiar but I didn't know why. Something fell across the photo, covering the sky, and I realized it was my sacred place, a Native American site in the bottom of the Grand Canyon. You, too, can find and create a sacred place in your mind, one that you imagine or one that you have seen, to connect you with your guides and angels.

For inspiration, research some of the many places around the world renowned for their healing powers and sacred energy. Among the best known are the spring at Lourdes in France, Stonehenge in England, and the Ganges River in India. Every year, millions of people pilgrimage to these and other sites in hope of Divine intervention to heal their ailments. Most leave with at least a sense of calm and acceptance; a number seem to receive miraculous healing. Angels, saints, or ancient gods are believed to inhabit these places. Here is a guide to some of them:

- **Lourdes, France.** In the mid-nineteenth century, a peasant girl named Bernadette had visions of the Virgin Mary appearing in a grotto of Massabiele near Lourdes, a village in the foothills of the

Pyrenees in southern France. She led others to the grotto, and a spring spontaneously appeared. The water is believed to have healing properties, drawing thousands of visitors each year.

- **Chartres Cathedral, France.** This Gothic cathedral built in the twelfth century contains the famous labyrinth with a rose at its center. It is believed to have been a Druid sacred site before the cathedral was built. The cathedral is dedicated to the Virgin Mary but is also believed to have many goddess origins.

- **Stonehenge, England.** Ancient circles of massive stones stand upright on a plain in England. They are believed to have spiritual or astronomical applications, or both, and it is still a mystery about who shaped, carried, and set the huge stones in place. Estimated to have been built between 2800 and 1400 B.C.E., Stonehenge is considered one of the Seven Wonders of the Ancient World.

- **The Pyramids, Egypt.** The Pyramids of Egypt rise up from the desert in the Giza plateau near the Nile River. They were burial vaults for the great pharaohs of Egypt, built about 2,700 B.C.E. Among them is the Great Sphinx, a sculpture with the head of a man and body of a lion. The Pyramids are also considered one of the Seven Wonders of the Ancient World.

- **Ganges River, India.** This river rising into the Himalayas is considered to be the most sacred river of Hinduism.

- **Medjugorge, Bosnia and Herzegovina.** Apparitions of the Virgin Mary have been seen here. As with Lourdes, thousands come each year seeking healing.

- **Chimayó, New Mexico.** Thousands flock throughout the year to Chimayó for its healing "holy dirt." On Good Friday, believers walk the road to Chimayó reenacting the walk of Christ carrying the cross. Some believers walk from as far as Albuquerque, nearly 100 miles away.

- **Sedona, Arizona.** The red cliffs of Sedona are thought to be one of the vortexes of the world, an entry point for higher spiritual wisdom to get through.

- **Glastonbury, England.** St. Michael's Tower appears on Tor, a giant hill that rises up from the emerald green fog-shrouded village, evoking the image of the mystical island Avalon shrouded in mist. Archangel Michael, traditionally regarded as the angel of light, the revealer of mysteries and guide to the other world, is believed to reside here. The area has strong associations with Arthurian legend and the quest for the Holy Grail.

- **Iona, Scotland.** One of the smaller islands of the Inner Hebrides, off the western coast of Scotland, Iona is only three and half miles long. It is thought to be a place where the veil between the material world and the Divine world is thinner. Geologically, it is strikingly different from neighboring islands. It is known for Iona marble, near-pristine white rock with streaks of celadon.

- **Chaco Canyon, New Mexico.** The site of ancient Native American ruins, from the height of Anasazi culture in the twelfth century. Like Stonehenge and other sacred stone sites, Chaco shows evidence that inhabitants lined up stones with the solstices and equinoxes.

- **Teotihuacan, Mexico.** Commonly translated from Nahuatl as "City of the Gods," these Aztec pyramids are sometimes called "the place where men become gods."

- **Angkor Wat, Cambodia.** The temples of Angkor were built from 879 to 1191, when the Khmer civilization was at its height. Suryavaram II built Angkor Wat in the twelfth century to honor the Hindu god Vishnu. To stand in its midst, it is said by some, is to be inspired by angelic grandeur and infinite possibility.

Certain angels are assigned to watch over specific sacred places. Choose for yourself a sacred place to use in your meditations. It could be one of the ones we have mentioned, or it could be another spot that resonates for you. Choose one of the angels from the lists in Chapter 10 to direct your focus in your next series of meditations. Ask your angel to inhabit your sacred place with you, to guard it and infuse it with Divine light and splendor.

Traveling Light

Angels are weightless, light beings. They carry no burdens. That is how some of us recognize them when we have angel encounters, as Lee Ann did that spring day in Brooklyn. She somehow sensed the angelic lightness of the man who hugged her, as did the others he greeted as they passed by. This weightlessness is vital to understanding the healing powers of angels. They bring *us* lightness. They restore us. In other words, they lift us into the light. Angels constantly implore us to surrender our burdens to the light. They remind us that the path to traveling weightless is forgiveness.

Angels can also signal to us when we need to take care of ourselves. They are the first to rush in to comfort us. They gently remind us to be just as generous to ourselves as we are to others. I am reminded of a talk I had with another healer who was concerned she was on the verge of a major health crisis. No physical signs lead her to worry. She had recently had a complete physical examination and received a clean bill of health. But she could not shake the persistent seed of worry. We talked about how of late she had experienced limitations on what she could give in healing sessions, but it was her fear that was creating the limitations. I showed her what she already was telling herself—that if she continued giving of her own energy constantly, she could bring on personal health problems. After our talk, she decided to set limits on how much she was personally giving and remember to channel the energy with the help of the healing guides and angels. This story reminds me of how necessary it is to be just as generous with ourselves as we sometime are with others. This woman's angel was telling her to slow down.

In a larger sense, we must be as generous in forgiving ourselves as we are with others. Much is written about the power of forgiving others to move through healing. Forgiving others for the hurts they have caused us can be powerful. As you forgive, ask your guides and angels to carry your wounds away, to make you new. Only when your hurts have been healed in your own eyes have you truly and completely forgiven. One of the final pieces of forgiveness, when we are committed to taking responsibility for our lives, is to forgive ourselves for letting it happen. Ask your angels and guides to release your wounds to the Universe, where your old hurts may rejoin the wholeness at the Source and reemerge to help the Universe. It is vital that you release the energy within you. Be gracious with yourself. This energy you hold serves no positive purpose and cannot serve a positive purpose for others. If it hurts you and continues to hurt you, it will hurt others.

The ultimate lesson all of us have to learn is unconditional love, which includes not only others but ourselves as well.
—Elisabeth Kübler-Ross, M.D. (1926–), Swiss psychiatrist and author

Grieving With Angels

When you have been hurt deeply, the burden is great. It might take a long time to grieve what you lost. Although you may have recovered—you may have learned to thrive through your surviving it—you might not be able to restore what you lost. The gentle spirits of angels can help you mourn your loss and move on.

Grief can weigh us down. Angels remind us to be light. Grief can be huge such as the death of a loved one, the end of a marriage. But it is important to also recognize the small losses in our lives as we walk through passages—from leaving a home, moving to a new place, losing a friend who is moving across the country, to changing jobs. Sometimes these griefs go unrecognized when they come to us as new opportunities. We are focused on the new place and all the excitement. But our angels can help us honor those passages.

There is a saying, "Wrestle the angel until it blesses you." This means to work with your grief and pain of conscience until you receive the blessing that allows you to go on—until you are released. Wrestling with the angel brings up the biblical story of Jacob, also known as Israel, the namesake of the Israel nation. In that story, Jacob wrestles all night with an angel. When the angel came to him, Jacob wasn't exactly the nicest guy in the world. He had just cheated his twin brother out of his birthright. During Jacob's struggle with God, he is marked—wounded in the leg with a limp he carried the rest of his life. But from that moment forward, Jacob walked in alignment with God, his conscious clear and his grief and fear cleansed. Jacob had accepted his assignment from God. It is said he never walked the same after that. He walked in the light.

Sometimes, we, too, are marked by our wrestling with the angels. Their angelic mark can be the blessing—a reminder that we don't have to wrestle with our darkness again.

Summoning Your Angels

Angels work on a mysterious schedule. They aren't summoned so much as they are welcomed. When we leave open spaces in our hearts, we can receive them. The veil between our material world and the higher side is lifted when we make ourselves receptive to what they offer. And timing is everything. The answers await you—when you are ready. Buddhist teacher Thich Nhat Hanh says all things can manifest if the conditions are right. The condition you *can* summon is the receptive state of your heart. Angels gently guide us to changing our hearts. Let them do their work, and one day you will see that a miraculous healing has taken place. A relationship you have worked for years to heal comes to a reconciliation. Pain stored in your body for decades gets released and freed.

> I shall light a candle of understanding in your heart, which shall not be put out.
> —*The Apocrypha*, 14:25

When we bow our heads and surrender to our Divine work, we don't always know where it will lead. Sometimes the catalyst is provided by the Divine or springs forth from a faith that cannot be explained. It's like a fountain that flows noiselessly from the Source. St. Teresa of Avila, a nun in sixteenth-century Spain who is celebrated as a master of mystical writing, spoke of the soul this way: Imagine there are two basins of water. In the first, the water comes from a great distance, through many elaborate conduits devised by human skill. This water flows with a spiritual sweetness that is produced by the sound of human meditation. The second basin, however, requires no conduit, as it has been constructed at the very source of the water and it fills spontaneously and noiselessly. We might work and work for years to fill the fountain, but one day, for no tangible reason, the fountain of healing flows within us from the Source and we are healed. St. Teresa also wrote, in *The Interior Castle*, of a crystal castle with seven chambers, each representing a different stage in the soul's spiritual quest for union with God. A woman ahead of her time, St. Teresa was persecuted most of her life by the Catholic Church for her belief that every person is capable of having a direct relationship with the Divine. Her teachings have recently found favor with contemporary audiences.

Light Works: Chapter 11 Angel Card

This chapter's angel card word is *Wholeness*. Health is a condition of balance and wholeness among the systems of your body as well as among your body, mind, and spirit. Your angel card for wholeness should represent this completeness. As you are working on this card, hold in your thoughts the sense of your own being—body, mind, and spirit—in health and wholeness. If you have an illness or injury, envision yourself healthy and whole. Use color, shapes, and images to create your angel card for *Wholeness*.

Highest and Best: A Healing Leap with the Angels

In the highest sense, angels close the gap between us and the Divine. They are the bridge that allows us to leap across to the open embrace of the Divine. Sometimes, when we are weak, they carry us across. Always, the aim is to make us whole—one with the Divine, one with each other, one with all our hurts and all our glories. We have seen Jacob wrestle with the angel, but we can also climb Jacob's Ladder, the stairway to heaven that the angels use to ascend and descend from the Source of All. Use this visualization anytime you need help from the angels to cross through travails and arrive safely on Divine ground:

1. Go to your sacred space or a place where you will not be disturbed.

2. Take three cleansing breaths, in through your nose and out through your mouth. Take a deep breath in through your nose to clear your body, and release it. Take a second breath to open your mind. Take a third breath to free your spirit.

3. Visualize yourself standing at the edge of a bridge. (We like the bridge leading to the Castel Sant'Angelo in Rome. It is trimmed with gold statues of angels who lead you across. It was named for a vision of Archangel Michael seen by Pope Gregory the Great in the sixth century as he led a procession across the bridge, praying for an end to the plague. Photos of it are available on the Internet or in travel books.) Or imagine you are at the foot of Jacob's Ladder.

4. In your mind's eye, populate your bridge with angels, kneeling and whispering gently to you. Envision them in flowing, gold-trimmed white robes and fluffy white wings.

5. Now imagine one of the angels stepping forward, beckoning to you with open arms. See yourself step forward.

6. Imagine the angel wrapping you in his or her gentle wings. Imagine yourself being led across the bridge protected by these gentle wings.

7. As you move across the bridge, see the light around you changing, transforming to pure white Light.

8. Now, you have reached the higher side. You are whole. You are healed. You are filled with Divine Light. You are among the angels at the Source.

The Sound of Trumpets

Angels are witness to our triumphs. They stand at the ready to trumpet our successes, to dress us in glory and light when we reach the center. Angels know our struggles. They are with us all the way, even through the paths that seem to torque and twist. They connect us to the Divine for healing. They open the window for us to release our pain. They allow the best in us to take wing.

Chapter 12

Being an Angel: Yes, *You!*

In *Empowering Your Life with Angels,* we have explored so many wonderful possibilities for connecting to your angels and spirit guides to welcome them into your daily experience and enrich your life through their Divine potential and joy. Throughout, though, we've also hinted at a greater and deeply personal possibility—one of connecting directly with your own Divine spiritual essence. We are *all* Divine. We are *all* of Spirit. We are *all* angels! Although we walk on the earth plane, as Elucia told us in her angel message given through my trance channel angel session in Chapter 3, we *do* possess the ability to access the realm of Spirit if we focus, concentrate, and allow Divine Spirit to fill and inspire us. It is not easy, but it can be done. So yes, you *can* touch the Divine— now, *today*—and remember the Source from which we all emerge and to which we all will return home after our adventures here on Earth are fulfilled.

Look in the mirror ... how do you feel when you see an angel looking back at you? Touch your angel face. How does it feel to be *face to face* with a genuine angel? Despite our human flaws and idiosyncrasies, if we look deeply enough into our own eyes, into our own hearts, we can recognize a vision of the Divine in ourselves and in others. In this chapter, as we complete our work together in *Empowering Your Life with Angels,* we will give you exercises to manifest your angel face and your angelic body and to meditate in prayer to reveal your angelic essence in communion with your angels and spirit guides.

This can be a surprisingly powerful and incredibly moving moment of connection with the Divine. You might feel vulnerable and revealed. This is okay and completely natural. Remember, you are one with the Divine, *you are safe, you are loved, and you are eternal.* Give yourself time to be with this realization, to absorb it, to embody the angelic in you. Join your angels and spirit guides as one among them, rejoicing in celebration of all that is. How would you feel and act differently if your angel nature was revealed in the face you present to yourself, to the world, *every day?* What would change if you moved about the world in an angel body? Let's ask the angels and spirit guides to help you reveal your angelic self, even as you acknowledge your unique and special contribution to the Divine, your own place in the great cosmos, and honor your choice to explore the Divine through human form. Let's begin with your angel cards.

Angel Card Inspiration

In each chapter of this book, we've created an angel card that features a word and an image along with a key concept for thinking about and meditating upon what it means to receive and accept that particular word and image in messages from your angels and guides and to send messages to them evoking that word and image. You will need to create one more angel card to complete the core collection of cards for your angel deck, and that's the one for this chapter.

Light Works: Chapter 12 Angel Card

This chapter's angel card words are *Celestial Self.* Your celestial self is your Divineness, the part of you that connects to the angelic. Your celestial self angel card should help you see and feel the strength, comfort, and love of this connection. Use color, shape, texture, and images to create an angel card that represents your *Celestial Self.* When you finish your card, hold it in your hands to infuse it with your energy—the energy of you, the angel.

Keep and use your angel card deck as you continue to empower your life with angels in the days and years to come. Laminate your cards to protect them so you will have them at the ready for your angel sessions and meditations. Gather your cards now and lay them out in an arc to represent the arc of an angel's wings, with the first and twelfth cards positioned at the tip of each wing. As you contemplate the cards, complete the following table with your personal impressions of the significance each angel card holds for you.

Angel Card from Chapter	Angel Card Word	General Meaning	Personal Meaning (Fill in for You)
1	*Oneness*	Synergistic and spiritual connections across boundaries of energy and form	_____ _____ _____
2	*Divine*	Our connections to the Divine energy of angels and guides and to the Divine as a whole	_____ _____ _____ _____
3	*Guidance*	Inspiration and direction; choosing whether to follow suggestions and advice	_____ _____ _____
4	*Essence*	The experience of angels and guides through the physical and psychic senses	_____ _____ _____
5	*Manifest*	Angels and their messages as they manifest, or come into tangible existence, in our lives	_____ _____ _____ _____
6	*Grace*	Acceptance of and gratitude for angels and guides and their messages and presence in our lives	_____ _____ _____ _____
7	*Forgiveness*	Releasing negativity to view challenges, problems, and difficult situations as gifts for personal growth and evolution	_____ _____ _____ _____ _____
8	*Intent*	The importance of purpose when traveling the path of communication between self-spirit and higher spirit	_____ _____ _____ _____

continues

continued

Angel Card from Chapter	Angel Card Word	General Meaning	Personal Meaning (Fill in for You)
9	*Wisdom*	Trusting in the answers; inner knowing applied to outer living	_____ _____ _____
10	*Bliss*	Following one's Divine path in life	_____ _____
11	*Wholeness*	The self (body, mind, and spirit) in balance	_____ _____
12	*Celestial Self*	The Divine you, your angelic essence	_____ _____

You can add to your angel card deck by creating additional cards for words that have special meaning for you in your communication with your angels and spirit guides. You might add a new angel card to your deck every month, for example, creating a card that embodies a spirit lesson you've learned recently or a concept that has taken on sudden and compelling personal significance for you in your life at this time. Draw or paint imagery on the card that visually captures the essence of what the word means to you for your life or just beautifully write the word. You might consider some of these words:

Peace	Comfort	Love	Joy
Compassion	Communication	Vision	Togetherness
Glory	Trust	Exchange	Explore
Community	Gratitude	Creativity	Power
Trust	Faith	Hope	Believe
Confidence	Strength	Comfort	Destiny
Balance	Healing	Path	Highest and Best
Light	Acceptance	Give	Receive
Connect	Support	Dream	Goal
Health	Grow	Transform	Inspire

Ways to Use Your Angel Cards

You can use your angel cards in limitless ways. They are wonderful tools for extending your ability to communicate with your angels and guides. They can stimulate your thoughts and help you focus your energy at the beginning of your angel sessions so you can ask the questions that concern you and open yourself to receiving the angels' answers. Use these ideas to get you started:

- **Five-minute morning meditation.** Each morning when you get up, choose an angel card. Meditate on the card for several minutes in a morning prayer. Let its imagery fill your thoughts and your mind and infuse your body with angelic light. Explore its colors, shapes, and design. Visualize the angel image or angel that comes to mind, and let that be your angel for the day.

- **Extended meditation.** Choose an angel card that you can take to your sacred place for a longer meditation. Look beyond the card itself to its meanings in your life at the moment.

- **Inspiration.** At any time during the day when negative feelings and images invade your consciousness, choose one of your angel cards. Focus on its word and imagery, and let it clear the negative energy from your thoughts and experience. Put the card on your desk or in a place where you can easily see it. Call on the angel Samandiriel to help you visualize your ideas and the angel Anahita to help you bring them to fruition.

- **Healing.** When you have a specific worry, concern, or health problem, hold your *Wholeness* or *Forgiveness* card in your hands and let its healing energy reach out to you. Use this energy to connect with Archangel Raphael, the Divine healer, and ask for his help with whatever ails you. Or call on some of the other angels of healing: Anael, Balthial, Gavreel, Mumiah, or Sariel.

- **Guidance.** Choose an angel card and use its energy to connect with the angels and guides that can help you with specific questions and concerns. For example, you might select the *Wisdom* angel card when you seek clarity as a means of reinforcing your connection to Archangel Uriel, the messenger of truth and insight, or some of the other angels associated with guidance listed in Chapter 10.

- **Connect with your personal angels and spirit guides.** Spread your angel cards out on the table, face up so you can see the images and read the words. One by one, choose cards that intuitively correspond to your angels and guides. Use the selected cards to help you focus your energy on linking to the angel or spirit guide and understanding the role each is given to bless your journey through this life.

In the Light: Outer Angel, Inner Angel

Look again at your angel cards, still spread out in an angel wing arc from card 1 at the top left wingtip to card 12 at the top right wingtip. Pick up each card individually, hold it, and meditate upon it. As you hold each card, meditate specifically upon whether that angel card resonates to the outer you, the person people see you to be in the world (and/or who you'd like them or *wish* them to see you to be ...), or whether the card better resonates to the inner you, the you carefully shielded and protected from earthly eyes and only perceived and recognized by your angels and spirit guides. If one card seems to resonate to both your inner and outer self, spend time to consider where you believe its influence is greater. As you make your decision about each card, place it in one of two piles, "Outer" or "Inner." Record your choices in the spaces provided. You might find that you have more cards resonating outward than *inward,* or vice versa, and that's okay. The important thing now is to be honest with yourself about where each card should go and put it where it holds the greater influence for you on your life journey at this moment.

Cards of Your Outer Angelic Self	Cards of Your Inner Angelic Self
_____	_____
_____	_____
_____	_____
_____	_____
_____	_____
_____	_____

Now, we'll take this exercise deeper into Spirit. Once again, lay out the cards as an arc of an angel's wingspan. This time, however, place the card you believe resonates to your most apparent *outward* angel quality at the top left tip of the wingspan. At the top right tip of the wingspan place the card you believe resonates to your most apparent *inward* angel quality. Then, fill in the angel arc by placing cards from left to right as they increasingly move your spirit from its outward resonance to its inward resonance. In other words, the cards move outward to inward from left to right. Record your choices here.

1. _____   12. _____

  2. _____   11. _____

    3. _____   10. _____

      4. _____   9. _____

        5. _____   8. _____

          6. _____   7. _____

As you look at your angel wing, meditate upon what the progression of cards reveals about your perception of the way you expose and protect your angelic essence. Consider each card and its "twin" on the opposite wing; how do the paired angel cards work with each other's energy? Are the pairs in, or out, of balance? Is there a truth in the totality of this angel card wingspan that surprises you? Are there cards you'd like to see change position? If the order of the cards was to change the direction of meaning, that is, if the top right card now represented your most outward quality and the top left your most inward quality, how would this change how other people see you and how you see yourself? As you discovered in the angel hologram meditation in Chapter 9, to "turn yourself inside out" can be transforming. Just as each point of light in a hologram provides a complete doorway to the whole, a view of the whole from its unique position and perspective, so does each angel card provide a unique entrance onto *you*—all of you! As you consider each angel card and how it uniquely informs who you are, let's move on to an exercise in which you will create your angel face.

The Countenance of the Divine

The countenance and body of an angel can be fierce and spectacular to behold. In previous chapters, we've explored how angels appear and what they are made of. Several Old Testament descriptions (New International Version) tell of angelic bearing and countenance:

- **Isaiah 6:2:** Above him were seraphs, each with six wings. With two wings they covered their faces, with two they covered their feet, and with two they were flying.

- **Ezekiel 10:12, 14:** Their entire bodies, including their backs, their hands, and their wings, were completely full of eyes, as were their four wheels. Each of the cherubim has four faces: One face was that of a cherub, the second the face of a man, the third the face of a lion, and the fourth the face of an eagle.

* **Daniel 10:5–6:** I looked up and there before me was a man dressed in linen, with a belt of the finest gold around his waist. His body was like chrysolite, his face like lightning, his eyes like gleaming torches, his arms and legs like the gleam of burnished bronze, and his voice like the sound of a multitude.

To create a connection from our human faces to the Divine, cultures and religions across time and around the globe have created masks to meld the actual and the perceived, the tangible and the representational, the real and the virtual, and the mundane and the Divine. As human beings, it seems we've always known, intuitively, that we become or that we are what we perceive. As Joseph Campbell writes in his timeless classic *The Masks of God: Primitive Mythology,* "Even though everyone knows that a man made the mask and that a man is wearing it ... the one wearing is identified with the god during the time of the ritual of which the mask is a part. He does not merely represent the god; he *is* the god." This presentation, Campbell notes, "... is allowed to work without correction upon the sentiments of both the beholder and the actor." In the exercises to come, I will ask you to create your angel mask, which will become a tangible representation of your own angelic countenance. Later, we will create your angelic body as well.

Once you have created your angel mask, you have a valuable tool to help you accept the reality of your essential angelic nature, one that bears your familiar earthly features yet embodies all your Divine yearnings and potential. Your reality becomes whatever your angelic mask represents about *you,* for the duration of the time the mask is *true to you* and during which you wear it. When you are the one wearing a mask, not only does the outside world see you in a certain way, but you also see the outside world with a particular focus. You are no longer *you;* instead, you *become* the Divine being—the fierce and spectacular countenance—your angel mask presents.

Ancient warriors across cultures, Western and Eastern, often donned masks for pre-battle rallies as they went to war, calling on the attributes of the gods and goddesses the masks represented to infuse the wearers with Divine courage and strength. Similarly summoned in the contexts of other ceremony and ritual were attributes such as love (the blessing of a marriage), longevity (the blessing of birth), and safe passage (the blessing of a journey), from the masks of their respective deities and

Divine angelic representatives. Actors in ancient Greek and Japanese theater wore masks to represent the essential truth of their characters, transcending the mundane identity of the players.

Just as you have begun to use your angel cards as a tool to understand your outward and inward angelic nature, you'll now use your angelic mask to illustrate and assume your angelic face. Your angel cards will further help guide you. You'll see!

About Face

People who know you and love you take comfort in the familiar features of your face—the shape of your cheeks, the curve of your smile, the boldness of your nose. Your face is your persona, your outward presentation. Sometimes it reveals and sometimes it hides who you are inside.

You might "put on a happy face" when you know that's what others expect of you, even when you feel frightened or sad or angry inside. Sometimes your face gives away your inner feelings of joy and happiness or of sadness and fear. You probably have a "business face" you use when you go to work. Whether you're an artist or a teacher, doctor or carpenter, computer expert or receptionist—whatever it is that you do for a living, your face is part of the "uniform" you put on. Your face, the outer you, supports your public image. In astrology, your ascendant, or rising, sign, is often thought to represent the face or mask you wear to the world, the self you want others to see.

The greatest revolution in our generation is that of human beings, who by changing the inner attitudes of their minds, can change the outer aspects of their lives.
—Marilyn Ferguson (1938–), American author

When you wear a mask—even figuratively the mask of your own face—you become what it presents. A mask becomes a way to connect the outer you and the inner you. In Chapter 7, I shared with you my wonderful experience with the girls at the adolescent treatment center where I worked as a counselor, who transformed themselves into an outward presentation of the angelic as they decorated themselves and their surroundings for a Christmas holiday celebration. These girls costumed themselves as angels and reflected outwardly the Divine being living within each of them. Their demeanors, their actions, and their faces all truly were those of the angelic.

What do you see when you envision the face of an angel? Is it the face of a beloved teacher, parent or grandparent, friend, or life partner? Is it an image brought back from meditation or prayer, a vision that appears when you need comforting, protection, or guidance? What does *your own* angel face look like? Sometimes, even when we can see the angelic in the faces of those who fill our lives, we have trouble imagining how we might appear as an angel to others—or how we might appear as an angel to ourselves!

Like Tarot's The Fool, about to set off on an archetypal journey from innocence to experience, get ready to explore *everything* about your angelic countenance and experience all this exploration allows and encourages.

Rita's painting of Tarot's Major Arcana card, The Fool.

Light Works: *Your* Angel Face

Set free your inhibitions and expectations! We're going to create the mask that is *your* angel face. This takes some time and planning, so you might want to read through all the directions first (here and in the later sections about decorating your mask) so you can gather the supplies you need and find a good place to work where you can let your angelic essence take flight and find expression (countenance!) through your angel mask. For the first part of making your angel mask, you'll probably want to have a friend help you.

Here's what you need to craft the mold of your angel mask:

- A friend who doesn't mind getting a little messy
- A place to work that also doesn't mind getting a little messy, like a kitchen or utility room or even outdoors if you can stay warm, dry, and out of the wind
- A package of cast bandage strips (most drug stores carry these; ask if you can't find them)
- A jar of petroleum jelly (such as Vaseline)
- A bowl of water big enough to hold the cast bandage strips
- Sharp scissors or a small, sharp knife
- Cleanup supplies: soap and water, facial cleanser if you prefer, washcloths, and towels

Messy is the key word for this adventure! If you're working at a table or countertop, cover the surface with plastic sheeting, old towels, or a drop cloth. Wear old clothes or a smock to protect your clothing. If you have long hair, pull it back from your face or cover it. You also will need to sit still for about 20 to 30 minutes, so have a comfortable chair nearby.

To make your mask:

1. Fill the bowl with water, and put it on the table.
2. Open the package of cast bandage, and lay out the strips.
3. Cover your face with petroleum jelly, forehead to chin to ears, including your lips but leaving your nostrils and eyes. Smear it on good. This is what keeps the plaster from sticking to your skin.
4. Have your friend place strips of cast bandage in the water and then apply them to your face over the petroleum jelly. Cover your entire face, forehead to chin and up to but not covering your ears, with the cast strips (except, of course, for your nostrils and eyes).
5. See that comfy chair? Have a seat and wait for the plaster to dry completely, which usually takes 20 to 30 minutes. You might need to tilt your head back to keep the mask from sliding out of position.
6. When the plaster is dry, have your friend help you carefully lift it from your face. Trim the rough edges with sharp scissors or a knife.

Put your mask in a safe place where it can dry for one to three days (longer is fine) without getting bumped around or splashed with water. Wash the petroleum jelly from your face with soap and water or facial cleanser. Did you get any plaster in your hair? It will easily wash out with warm water and shampoo. If any plaster has gotten onto surfaces such as the table or floor, wipe it with a cloth moistened with warm water. If it resists coming up, leave it to dry the rest of the way and then gently scrape it to remove it.

When your mask is completely dry, decorate your mundane expression with your angelic countenance!

When we discover that the truth is already in us, we are all at once our original selves.
—Dogen (1200–1253), founder of Soto Zen

Light Works: The Features of Your Angel Face

You'll be decorating your angel mask on three layers:

- The *exterior* of the mask, which is the outer countenance of an angel that others behold, react to, and relate with
- The *interior* of the mask, which is the hidden, protected expression only you and your angels and spirit guides behold, although some of those closest to you might have received the privilege of a peak at the visage that rests there
- The *interface,* or connection between your inner and outer angelic selves, the interior and exterior of the mask

For help decorating your angel mask, we're going to turn again to your angel cards you earlier divided into those resonating to the outer you and those resonating to the inner you. Place the angel cards once again in their positions from outward to inward as you recorded them earlier in this chapter. Keep this wingspan in view as you begin to decorate your mask; I'll ask you to work with the cards in specific ways as you define and embody each layer of your angel countenance.

You can use all sorts of materials to create the features of your angel mask. And remember, this is your *angel* face. Its appearance doesn't have to fit with convention. You can decorate your mask with just about anything that captures your sense of creativity. To get your imagination started, consider some of the following materials:

- Acrylic paints applied with brushes, other objects, or your fingers
- Sequins and glitter
- Feathers
- Yarn, ribbon, and colored string
- Buttons and beads
- Costume jewelry
- Copper wire or other metal objects
- Stones and crystals
- Colored tiles (You can even carefully break an old plate and use the pieces.)
- Pieces of fabric or handmade paper
- Photographs
- Items from nature such as dried flowers or materials that represent your animal totems

You'll need glue to attach materials to your mask. You might also want scissors; a hammer if you'd like to crush stones, crystals, or tiles; and a nail or pointed object if you want to push items into or weave them through your mask. Here are some additional hints and tips for decorating:

- Although your plaster creation is fairly sturdy, it can crack or break with pressure. Do you have any plaster strips left over? If so, you can use them for quick repairs. Simply apply a strip to the area of damage in the same way you put the strips together when you were first making your mask. You can work around this area while it dries or set your mask aside overnight and come back to it.

- Water-based paints will soften the plaster while they are wet, which might cause the plaster to begin mixing with the paint. This can create some different and interesting patterns, if you like the effect. If you don't, wait for the paint and plaster to dry and then reapply the paint with single brush strokes to lay down solid colors or apply gesso or clear acrylic gel medium over the raw mask (get these sealant products at art supply stores).

- Because plaster softens when it's wet, a drop or two of water is all you need if you want to "implant" objects in your mask or to push items through it. Place a small drop of water at the site, wait a few minutes for the plaster to begin to dissolve, then carefully guide your object into or through the site.

- If you want to do patterns such as stars or moons, use a pencil to softly outline your design or pattern.

- If you have trouble getting glued items to stay put, place a spot of glue where you want to attach an item and wait for the spot to dry. This seals the plaster. Then apply more glue and the item, hold for a few minutes until the item remains in place, then allow the glue to thoroughly dry.

The Colors of Your Angelic Self

Consider how you want to use color as you decorate the three layers of your angel mask. Do you want to leave one or more of the layers white? Certainly you can! White has its unique representations, both spiritually and to each of us personally. Angels and angelic representations universally have certain colors associated with them. You can apply some of these common color associations to your mask if you wish. However, the way in which you use color as you decorate your angel mask is highly personal, and if you resonate to a particular color, use it. The most important thing to remember is to use whatever colors appeal and feel right to *you*.

Color	Representations	Angel Associations
Black	Protection, solidarity, banishing the negative; Scorpio; Saturn	Barakiel, angel of fire; Cassiel, angel of determination; Mihael, angel of trustworthiness; Vohamanah, angel of optimism
Blue	Patience, tranquility, intuition, transformation; Cancer, Libra, Pisces, Sagittarius, Taurus; Venus, Moon	Colopatiron, angel of liberation; Ezekiel, angel of dynamic existence; Valoel, angel of tranquility and inner peace
Brown	Friendship, kindness to animals, the energy of Planet Earth, financial soundness; Virgo, Aquarius	Asmodel, angel of common sense; Hamaliel, angel of order; Liwet, angel of original ideas; Maion, angel of self-discipline; Mihr, angel of friendship

Color	Representations	Angel Associations
Gold	Masculine energy, confidence, courage; Leo; Sun	Rampel, angel of endurance; Raphael, angel of health and life; Sandalphon, angel of strength and courage
Green	Health, fertility, growth, joy; prosperity, money, nature; Pisces, Taurus; Venus, Jupiter	Anael, angel of love; Anahita, angel of fertility; Barakiel, angel of good fortune; Lailah, angel of conception
Grey	Neutrality, balance; Libra; Saturn, Venus	Chamuel, angel of tolerance; Shekinah, angel of emotional and spiritual balance; Soqed Hozi, angel of balance in relationships; Zuriel, angel of harmony
Orange	Encouragement, valor, ability to manifest; Aquarius, Leo, Virgo; Mercury, Sun	Aamaita, angel of wisdom of the heart; Michael, angel of protection; Verchiel, angel of generosity
Pink	Love, compassion, goodness; Libra, Taurus; Venus	Anael, angel of sexuality and romantic love; Muriel, angel of emotions; Ongkanon, angel of truth in sharing deep feelings; Sammael, angel of romance and marriage
Purple	Healing, success, ambition, career and business aspirations; Sagittarius; Jupiter, Mercury	Anauel, angel of success and prosperity; Barakiel, angel of good fortune; Casseil, angel of business acumen; Sachiel, angel of affluence
Red	Passion, longevity, victory, success, strength; Aries, Leo, Scorpio; Mars	Abdiel, angel of courage in adversity; Perpetiel, angel of victory; Mumiah, angel of longevity; Uriel, angel of artistic passion
Silver	Feminine energy, compassion, spiritual wisdom; Cancer, Virgo; Moon	Ardoustus, angel of nurturing; Gazardiel, angel of enlightenment; Rhamiel, angel of empathy; Zagzagel, angel of inner wisdom

continues

continued

Color	Representations	Angel Associations
White	Truth, hope, protection, miracles, purity, Divine love, the Divine; Cancer; Moon	Hadraniel, angel of Divine love Hamied, angel of Divine intervention; The Virtues, angels of miracles; Ananchel, angel of Divine love
Yellow	Confidence, travel, intellect, creativity; Leo; Mercury, Sun	Afriel, angel of exploration; Dina, angel of learning; Gabriel, angel of travel; Harahel, angel of new ideas

Your Outer Angel Face

With the angel cards for your outward angel self to guide you, begin to decorate the exterior of your mask, the side that faces those who will see you when you wear this mask. From your angel card wingspan, pull out the cards resonating to your outer self that are most important and inspirational to your task at hand. Also choose the one card from the inner wing that you would most like to see move to a new position on the outer wing. You will want to be sure that the words for the angel qualities you have selected are evoked through the colors and imagery you choose for this outer layer of your angel face. You might even want to paint one of the angel card words on the mask itself.

While you are working, allow yourself the freedom to form whatever countenance beams true to you. Remember the Old Testament descriptions quoted earlier in this chapter where the angel face contained many eyes. An angel's face is allegorical, that is, symbolic or figurative. The images you create and the materials you use can be as fantastical as you desire. Consider using copper wire to attach symbols in a halolike fashion at the top of the mask—from the sun, moon, and stars, to whatever icons and images hold meaning to you—for all the world to see. Or perhaps you want to morph the shape of your angel face to include the radiating rays of the sun or to take the shape of a new moon with all its inherent new beginnings and potentials.

Central to this experience is that you decorate all the layers of your angel mask *intuitively*. Whether you work quickly or slowly makes no difference, just be sure to work from your heart. Before you begin a decorating session, use this affirmation to enlist the aid of your angels and spirit guides to help you move cathartically toward manifesting the Divine upon your outward angel features:

Angels and spirits, guide my hand and my heart as I work to manifest my outward angel self. May this outer countenance light the path to the highest and best for me and for all who look upon this angel vision.

Take special care in decorating the Third Eye of the outward layer of your angel mask. This sacred portal allows the Divine to access your inner angel layer. The way you choose to show your Third Eye to the world can reveal much about how accessible you are to Spirit and how open you are to allow the Divine to come with welcome into your being.

Your Inner Angel Face

Now, let's turn your attention to the inner layer of your angel mask. This is the side of the mask that touches your human face and in a way becomes the bond between your mundane self on the earth plane and your inner celestial angel being of light. Your guiding spirits and angels do see this inner you because your angels see all that you are. So ask your angels and guides to help you decorate this interior, intimate layer that is the inside of your angel mask.

Begin by looking at the angel card wingspan you set aside to resonate with your inner and outer Divine self. Look particularly at the inner cards you feel have most relevance to guide you in decorating the inner layer of your mask. Do you want to continue the same colors and designs from the angel cards, or do you want to do something totally different? Whatever *feels* right to you *is* right, so follow your inner artist and the guidance of your angels. Think, too, as you're decorating the inside of your mask, about how it will feel to have this interior of your angel face touching your own face. Chose one angel card from the outer wing of the wingspan that represents one quality you'd like to enhance inwardly, and allow this card to inform your creative work as well.

How does this inner layer resonate to the outer layer of your angel mask? If the exterior is the sun, is the interior the moon? Or is the exterior yin to an interior yang? When outer and inner become mirrors of each other, what is seen, reflected, and revealed? Images may continue front to back as they are reinterpreted on each side of the mask to express on one side the outer and on the other side the inner countenance. The difference between outer and inner might become one of texture for you, with rough surfaces on one side and smooth, even surfaces on the other. The very shape of the mask might change as each side is viewed.

Use this affirmation to enlist the aid of your angels and spirit guides to help you move cathartically toward manifesting the Divine upon your inward angel features:

Angels and spirits, guide my hand and my heart as I work to manifest my inward angel self. May this inner countenance inspire my outer thoughts, words, and deeds, to the highest and best for my life and the lives of all who share its light.

As you decorated the Third Eye on the outer layer of your mask, so you will decorate it for this inner layer. Here you show how the Divine touches the skin of your face, how you allow this Divine portal to blossom, filling your body with celestial light. Are you open or closed? Are you clogged or bejeweled?

The Space Between: Your Angel Interface

There's one final layer, or dimension, to decorating the face of the angel that is you: the connection between the inner angel countenance and the outer angel countenance. How do your inner and outer angel selves merge? You may have already punctured the plaster to carry objects through the mask, from outside to inside or from inside to outside. Or you might feel that your mask is complete, now, that it represents this merging as it is—and that's fine. Look one more time at the edge of your mask, where its outer and inner boundaries meet. Is there more decorating work to do here? Can you find ways to represent the places upon which your outer and inner angel faces touch? As you consider your angel interface, look closely at the two angel cards in your angel wingspan that represent your most outer and inner angel selves. As you meditate upon the resonance of these two angel qualities, consider whether you have manifested their intersection at the interface of your mask.

Use this affirmation to enlist the aid of your angels and spirit guides to help you move cathartically toward manifesting the Divine upon the interface of your angel features:

Angels and spirits, guide my hand and my heart as I work to manifest the Divine interface of outer and inner angelic countenance. May this connection of Divine energy guide my being to the harmony and sacred balance of the highest and best for my life and for the aid of other beings here on Earth and in Spirit.

Once again we return to the Third Eye. Look at how your outward and inward manifestations of this portal inform and resonate together. Is there more work to be done here at the energetic interface to show or to maximize the power of this Divine portal without and within your angel being?

Countenance of an Angel

Now that your mask is finished and completely dry, hold it in your hands. Take your mask to a sacred place where there is a mirror or bring a mirror to your sacred place. Look first at your own face in the mirror. Then put your angel mask to your face. Allow the interior of the mask to touch your skin. Become. Behold. *You are an angel.* Use the mask in your sessions to deepen your work with your angels and spirit guides.

Highest and Best: Your Angel Body

You have fully manifested your angelic countenance, so now we'll add your angelic body as well. Have you ever made a snow angel? I encourage you to create your angel body outdoors if you can do so—in the snow, in the sand on the beach, even in a bed of long grass or a meadow. Take with you your angel mask and your angel cards as well as any other important talismans you might want to use to decorate your angel body.

1. First, lie in the snow, sand, or grass and make an impression to form the body of your angel, moving your arms to create the wingspan. If you can't do this activity outdoors, get a large piece of butcher paper and tape it out flat on the floor. Lie down and have someone trace your outline. Then do the rest of the exercise using your tracing. Draw or paint wings on your form.

2. Place your angel mask at the head of the angel. Then place your angel cards around the body wherever it is you feel the word on each card belongs. Secure each card to the angel body with a found item, such as a stone or branch, or use a crystal or other weighty object of importance and meaning to you. Place the two angel cards you've chosen as your most outer and inner angel qualities on the left and right wingtips respectively. Take special care as you decorate and define your angel wings. Continue to decorate your angel body with whatever you have brought with you or with whatever you find in your environment and surroundings until you are satisfied with this complete angel being.

3. Take a photograph with a conventional or digital camera to pre-serve this angel image, and use this manifestation of your angel countenance and body for meditation and guidance. If you like, use the image to create another card for your angel deck.

Stand and view your angel being—its countenance and bearing fierce and spectacular to behold. Repeat this affirmation:

My angels, I am one with you in Spirit for the highest and best of All.

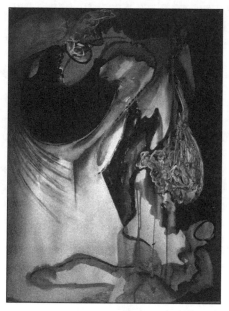

Rita's painting of Celestial Spirit, Birth.

You Are Divine

Each one of us is a Divine being who comes to this earth to learn and remember our Divine purpose. As the angelic being Elucia reminds us in Chapter 3, *you may wonder, but you know.* I wish you joy as you redis-cover all there is to know about your Divine celestial self, your angels, your guides in Spirit, and the great Source that inspires and creates all that was, all that is, all that will be. Breathe, live life, and know you are in and of the Divine. Remember, you are an angel here on Earth.

Appendix A

Angels of the Hours

According to some medieval practices, the first hour of each day begins with sunrise, and the angel of that hour is the angel of the day. The seven daily angels then rotate through the hours of each day, taking turns as the angel of the hour. The following table presents the clean and simple version: The time of sunrise identifies the hour of the day and its corresponding angel. For example, if on Sunday, March 16, sunrise is at 6:14 A.M., then the first hour of the day is 6 A.M. The angel of Sunday is Michael, who is the angel of the first hour of the day—6 A.M. to 7 A.M. The angels of the hours always rotate in the same order, although the angel of the first hour changes each day. Which angel of the hour begins your day today? Which angel guides you now, at this hour?

Use the following tables to access the energy and divine inspiration of the angel for each and every important hour that looms large and small in your life. This could be the hour of your wedding, your child's piano recital, your dentist appointment, dinner with your best friend, or the joy of snuggling up with your partner as you drift off to sleep. Or call on the angels of the hours to empower you all day (and night) long!

Angels of the Hours

Michael	Master protector and guardian
Gabriel	Nurturing, creativity, and messenger of good news
Sammael	Emotions and life passion
Raphael	Healing, travel, and communication
Zachariel	Release from material attachments
Anael	Romantic passion
Cassiel	Social order and business endeavors

Hour of the Day	Sunday	Monday	Tuesday	Wednesday	Thursday	Friday	Saturday
1st	Michael	Gabriel	Sammael	Raphael	Zachariel	Anael	Cassiel
2nd	Anael	Cassiel	Michael	Gabriel	Sammael	Raphael	Zachariel
3rd	Raphael	Zachariel	Anael	Cassiel	Michael	Gabriel	Sammael
4th	Gabriel	Sammael	Raphael	Zachariel	Anael	Cassiel	Michael
5th	Cassiel	Michael	Gabriel	Sammael	Raphael	Zachariel	Anael
6th	Zachariel	Anael	Cassiel	Michael	Gabriel	Sammael	Raphael
7th	Sammael	Raphael	Zachariel	Anael	Cassiel	Michael	Gabriel
8th	Michael	Gabriel	Sammael	Raphael	Zachariel	Anael	Cassiel
9th	Anael	Cassiel	Michael	Gabriel	Sammael	Raphael	Zachariel
10th	Raphael	Zachariel	Anael	Cassiel	Michael	Gabriel	Sammael
11th	Gabriel	Sammael	Raphael	Zachariel	Anael	Cassiel	Michael
12th	Cassiel	Michael	Gabriel	Sammael	Raphael	Zachariel	Anael
13th	Zachariel	Anael	Cassiel	Michael	Gabriel	Sammael	Raphael
14th	Sammael	Raphael	Zachariel	Anael	Cassiel	Michael	Gabriel
15th	Michael	Gabriel	Sammael	Raphael	Zachariel	Anael	Cassiel
16th	Anael	Cassiel	Michael	Gabriel	Sammael	Raphael	Zachariel
17th	Raphael	Zachariel	Anael	Cassiel	Michael	Gabriel	Sammael
18th	Gabriel	Sammael	Raphael	Zachariel	Anael	Cassiel	Michael
19th	Cassiel	Michael	Gabriel	Sammael	Raphael	Zachariel	Anael
20th	Zachariel	Anael	Cassiel	Michael	Gabriel	Sammael	Raphael
21st	Sammael	Raphael	Zachariel	Anael	Cassiel	Michael	Gabriel
22nd	Michael	Gabriel	Sammael	Raphael	Zachariel	Anael	Cassiel
23rd	Anael	Cassiel	Michael	Gabriel	Sammael	Raphael	Zachariel
24th	Raphael	Zachariel	Anael	Cassiel	Michael	Gabriel	Sammael

Appendix B

Resources

There certainly is no shortage of information available on the topic of angels! The challenge is more deciding where to go next as you continue to explore your interest in angels. Some of the resources in this appendix are materials referenced in the book. Others are additional sources to help you satisfy your curiosity and expand your knowledge.

Books and Audiocassettes

These books and other materials are good sources for additional information about angels and spirit guides.

Berkowitz, Rita S., and Deborah S. Romaine. *The Complete Idiot's Guide to Communicating with Spirits.* Indianapolis: Alpha Books, 2002.

Brennan, Barbara Ann. *Hands of Light: A Guide to Energy Healing Through the Human Energy Field.* New York: Bantam, 1988.

Brown, Sylvia. *Sylvia Brown's Book of Angels.* Carlsbad, CA: Hay House, 2003.

———. *Angels and Spirit Guides* (audiocassette). Carlsbad, CA: Hay House, 1999.

Budilovsky, Joan, and Eve Adamson. *The Complete Idiot's Guide to Meditation, Second Edition*. Indianapolis: Alpha Books, 2002.

Carey, Jacqueline. *Angels: Celestial Spirits in Legend and Art*. New York: Metro Books, 1997.

Chearney, Lee Ann, ed. *The Quotable Angel: A Treasury of Inspiring Quotations Spanning the Ages*. New York: John Wiley & Sons, 1995.

Chodron, Pema. *The Places that Scare You: A Guide to Fearlessness in Difficult Times*. Boston: Shambhala Publications, 2002.

Chopra, Deepak. *The Path to Love: Spiritual Strategies for Healing*. New York: Three Rivers Press, 1998.

Daniel, Alma, Timothy Wyllie, and Andrew Ramer. *Ask Your Angels: A Practical Guide to Working with the Messengers of Heaven to Empower and Enrich Your Life*. New York: Ballantine Books, 1992.

Davidson, Gustav. *A Dictionary of Angels Including the Fallen Angels, Reissue Edition*. New York: The Free Press, 1994.

Edward, John. *Understanding Your Angels and Meeting Your Guides* (audiocassette). Carlsbad, CA: Hay House, 2000.

Fox, Sabrina. *Loved by Angels: Angels Are Right Beside Us, Even If We Don't Yet See Them*. Nashville, TN: Bluestar Communication, 1999.

Grubb, Nancy. *Angels in Art*. New York: Artabras, 1995.

Guiley, Rosemary Ellen. *Encyclopedia of Angels, Reprint Edition*. New York: Checkmark Books, 1998.

Kübler-Ross, Elisabeth. *On Death and Dying, Reprint Edition*. New York: Scribner and Sons, 1997.

Küstenmacher, Marion, and Werner Küstenmacher. *Mandalas for Power and Energy*. New York: Sterling Publishing Co., 2003.

Lewis, James R., and Evelyn Dorothy Oliver. *Angels A to Z*. Canton, MI: Visible Ink Press, 1996.

Mark, Barbara, and Trudy Griswold. *The Angelspeake Book of Prayer and Healing*. New York: Simon & Schuster, 1997.

———. *The Angelspeake Storybook*. Avon, MA: Adams Media Corporation, 2000.

Myss, Caroline. *Sacred Contracts: Awakening Your Divine Potential*. New York: Harmony Books, 2002.

O'Neill, Kim. *How to Talk with Your Angels*. New York: Avon Books, 1995.

Van Praagh, James. *Meditations with James Van Praagh*. New York: Fireside, 2003.

———. *Reaching to Heaven: A Spiritual Journey Through Life and Death*. New York: Penguin, 1999.

Virtue, Doreen. *Archangels and Ascended Masters: A Guide to Working and Healing with Divinities and Deities*. Carlsbad, CA: Hay House, 2003.

———. *Healing with the Angels: How the Angels Can Assist You in Every Area of Your Life*. Carlsbad, CA: Hay House, 1999.

———. *Messages from the Angels: What Your Angels Want You to Know*. Carlsbad, CA: Hay House, 2003.

White, Ruth. *Working with Your Guides and Angels*. Boston: Weiser Books, 1997.

Inspiration and Oracle Cards

You've made your own personalized set of angel cards to use for inspiration and meditation. Here are some of the most popular decks of cards you can buy in book stores, spiritual stores, and metaphysical stores.

Angel Blessings: Cards of Sacred Guidance and Inspiration by Kimberly Marooney

ANGEL Cards by Kathy Tyler and Joy Drake

Angel Meditations by Sonia Cafe

Angel of Light Cards by Diana Cooper

Archetype Cards by Caroline Myss

Harmony Angel Cards by Angela McGerr

Healing Cards by Caroline Myss

Healing with Angels Oracle Cards by Doreen Virtue

Healing with the Fairies Oracle Cards by Doreen Virtue

Magical Spell Cards by Lucy Cavendish

Manifesting Good Luck Cards by Deepak Chopra

Messages from Your Angels Oracle Cards by Doreen Virtue

Self-Care Cards by Cheryl Richardson

Movies

Angels have captivated movie audiences from the earliest films. Most of these are available for rental or purchase on DVD or video. It's fun to watch the original and its remakes to see how our perceptions of angels have changed through the decades (Chapter 5 tells you which movies have remakes).

Almost an Angel (1990)

Angels in America (2003)

Angels in the Outfield (1951, 1994)

The Bishop's Wife (1947)

City of Angels (1998)

Date with an Angel (1987)

Dogma (1999)

Down to Earth (2001)

Faraway, So Close! (1993)

Heaven Can Wait (1978)

Heaven Only Knows (1947)

The Heavenly Kid (1985)

Here Comes Mr. Jordan (1941)

I Married an Angel (1942)

It's a Wonderful Life (1946)

A Life Less Ordinary (1997)

Michael (1996)

The Preacher's Wife (1996)

The Prophecy (1995); *The Prophecy II* (1998)

What Dreams May Come (1998)

Wings of Desire (1987)

Music Composers/Recording Artists/ Record Labels

Put on some angelic music when you meditate or while doing some of the exercises in this book to help you focus your thoughts and your spiritual energy.

Aeoliah

David Arkenstone

Johann Sebastian Bach

Ludwig von Beethoven

Johannes Brahms

Erik Berglund

Jim Brickman

Philip Chapman

Cusco

Alex De Grassi

Deuter

Herb Ernst

Medwyn Goodall

Steven Halpern

George Frideric Handel

Inner Peace Music

David Lanz

Wolfgang Amadeus Mozart

New World Music

Johann Pachelbel

Narada Productions

Mike Rowland

Antonio Vivaldi

Windham Hill Records

George Winston

Websites

There are thousands of Internet resources dealing with angels. Here are a few to get you started on your quest for more information.

www.angelcsc.com

This website lists certified spiritual counselors (CSCs) and angel therapy practitioners (ATPs) by state and country.

www.angeltherapy.com

The website for spiritual clairvoyant and psychologist Dr. Doreen Virtue includes articles, daily meditations, and information about Dr. Virtue's books, tapes, oracle cards, and appearances.

www.elisabethkublerross.com

The website for Dr. Elisabeth Kübler-Ross, psychiatrist (now retired) and author of the watershed book *On Death and Dying* first published in 1969 contains articles, resources, and thought-provoking quotes.

www.ofspirit.com

This online magazine features more than 1,000 pages of spiritual articles and information on topics from acupuncture to mediums to Zen ... and everything in between.

www.thespiritartist.com

The website for author Rita Berkowitz features articles and information about Rita's work as a spiritual counselor and psychic artist and displays some of Rita's amazing spirit drawings.

www.soulstirring.org
The website features the work of, and links to, artists, musicians, and performers whose works are spiritual or mystic.

Index

The New Age Way
to Get What You Want Out of Life

Empowering Your Life with Wicca
ISBN: 0-02-864437-9
$14.95 US/$22.99 CAN

Empowering Your Life with Dreams
ISBN: 1-59257-092-5
$14.95 US/$22.99 CAN

Empowering Your Life with Joy
ISBN: 1-59257-097-6
$14.95 US/$22.99 CAN

Empowering Your Life with Runes
ISBN: 1-59257-165-4
$14.95 US/$22.99 CAN

Empowering Your Life with Yoga
ISBN: 1-59257-249-9
$14.95 US/$22.99 CAN

ISBN: 1-59257-268-5
$14.95 US/$22.99 CAN

ISBN: 1-59257-207-3
$14.95 US/$22.99 CAN

ISBN: 1-59257-236-7
$14.95 US/$22.99 CAN